Loch Lomond
and the
Trossachs

40 Favourite Walks

D1376416

The author and publisher have made every effort to ensure that the information in this publication is accurate, and accept no responsibility whatsoever for any loss, injury or inconvenience experienced by any person or persons whilst using this book.

published by
pocket mountains ltd
The Old Church, Annanside,
Moffat, Dumfries and Galloway DG10 9HB
pocketmountains.com

ISBN: 978-1-907025-04-4

A catalogue record for this book is available from the British Library

All route maps are based on 1945 Popular Edition Ordnance Survey material and revised from field surveys by Pocket Mountains Ltd, 2009. © Pocket Mountains Ltd 2010.

Printed in Poland

Introduction

Loch Lomond is the largest freshwater expanse in mainland Britain and despite its easy accessibility it remains one of the most beautiful. Its 'Bonnie Banks', as celebrated in the romantic ballad, are clothed with native oakwoods, a fantastic habitat for wildlife and ideal for family walks.

To the east are the Trossachs, a compact huddle of rocky hills, dense forests and jewel-like smaller lochs that have been dubbed the 'Highlands in Miniature'. It was Sir Walter Scott's poem *Lady of the Lake*, set on Loch Katrine, and his novel based on the life of Rob Roy that first made the area famous, and it remains a favourite on many itineraries of Scotland.

West of Loch Lomond, the scene changes; here, clustered around the head of Loch Long, rise a group of mountains so steep and rocky that they have become known as the Arrochar Alps. The Rest and Be Thankful pass gives access to the Cowal Peninsula, now somewhat neglected but once a favourite for holidaying Glaswegians who came here in the age of the steamers.

Together these landscapes make up Scotland's first National Park, recognising the importance of this natural breathing space so close to Glasgow and yet so apart, and the need to protect it from the pressures of visitor numbers and insensitive development.

How to use this guide
This guide contains 40 short to moderate walks, most of which can be undertaken in

half a day, exploring the area's varied terrain.

With good connections to Glasgow and Stirling, many of the walks are accessible by bus, although timetables should be checked at the local tourist information centre or online at traveline.org.uk as school holiday and last-minute timetable changes are possible.

Ferries and pleasure boats on Loch Lomond and Loch Katrine make a pleasant alternative to road transport; there is even the chance to hire your own boat from Balmaha Boatyard to visit Inchcailloch Island.

Many of these walks are on forestry tracks or prepared paths, and mention is made when the terrain is particularly boggy, steep or rocky. However, bear in mind that ground conditions can be as changeable as the weather and most of the walks will require waterproof footwear. The higher peaks can often be snow covered in winter, making their ascent a much more serious proposition.

While a sketch map accompanies each walk, it is always useful to have an OS map with you, even perhaps on waymarked trails, in case you stray from the route or need to shortcut to safety. Waterproofs should be carried on all except the shortest routes, and the mountain climbs require full hillwalking clothing, a map and navigation skills.

Due to the rugged terrain, only a few of the walks are suitable for all-terrain baby buggies and these are highlighted at the start of the relevant route. However, there are a number of walks which are especially child friendly, with the inclusion of a boat trip (Loch Katrine, Inchcailloch Island, and Inversnaid RSPB Trail), the chance to watch red squirrels and birds from the comfort of a wildlife hide (Glenbranter, Puck's Glen, and the Lime Craig Circuit), or a hunt for sculptures and other riddles hidden in the forest (Loch Ard and Lochan Spling). Many other walks provide perfect picnic spots and the chance to cool off with a paddle in lochs or burns.

The Land Reform (Scotland) Act 2003 gave walkers the right of access over most Scottish land away from residential buildings. With this right comes responsibilities, as set out in the Scottish Outdoor Access Code: these include respect for other land users and responsible access, especially on farmed and grazing land. In particular, dogs should be kept on tight leads during the spring and early summer to stop them disturbing ground-nesting birds and livestock. Dogs should also be kept well away from sheep with lambs at all times. Deer stalking takes place on the hills between 1 July and 20 October, but this should not usually conflict with any of the walks described in this guide as long as you stick to the recommended route. Ticks and midges can sometimes be a hazard during the summer months: the best precautions are to cover up, wear light-coloured clothing, use insect repellent and check and remove ticks each day.

History

The area has a rich history and landscape which has in turn inspired writers, artists and poets. The outlaw Rob Roy MacGregor became famous in his own lifetime. Born near the head of Loch Katrine, he lived for many years by Balquhidder. Along with his father, he took part in the Jacobite rising and was badly injured at the Battle of Glen Shiel in 1719. His family were evicted from their lands and their house burnt to the ground by the Duke of Montrose, driving Rob Roy to live as an outlaw, waging a personal feud against the Duke and passing into legend as the Scottish Robin Hood. His public popularity meant that although imprisoned, he was eventually pardoned by King George I just before he was due to be transported to the colonies. He died in his house at Inverlochlarig Beg, Balquhidder, on 28 December 1734.

Sir Walter Scott later penned a bestselling novel based on Rob Roy's story in 1817, and Wordsworth wrote a poem entitled 'Rob Roy's Grave' during a visit to the area in 1803. These events heralded the romanticising of Loch Lomond and the Trossachs as artists such as Millais and the critic John Ruskin also drew inspiration from the landscape. By the mid-1800s, the area was a firm feature on the Grand Tour.

Recreation of a different type was gaining pace on the other side of Loch Lomond, as the Arrochar Alps became popular as a climbers' playground from the 1890s on. Traditionally the preserve of well-to-do gentlemen, by the 1930s a new group of climbers, the unemployed and the working class from the shipyards and factories of Glasgow, came to the area by bike, foot, bus and train to hone their climbing skills on the many peaks, sleeping in howffs under boulders, with the rockfaces of the Cobbler becoming a firm favourite.

The natural environment

This area lies across the Highland Boundary Fault, a wide crumple-zone caused by two different types of rock crashing against each other. The north and west is made up of hard metamorphic rock, with softer sandstones, conglomerates and sedimentary rocks making up the south and east. The faultline was particularly active 400-500 million years ago when the region was rocked by regular earthquakes. The geology has since settled down, but the fault still forms a dividing line between the Highlands and Lowlands of Scotland: one of the best views of the effect of the faultline can be seen from the summit of Conic Hill by Balmaha.

It is this geology which gives the Trossachs its distinct character. Also described as Scotland's Lake District, the area is divided by small wooded peaks and hills with many picturesque lochs dotted in between. The bustling settlements of Callander and Aberfoyle, important wool-trading markets in the past, in addition to smaller villages often with cafés or inns, make this an ideal area for pleasant touring without having to travel many miles each day.

Newer industries have taken advantage of the geography, with forestry becoming very important in places. Two expanses of forestry dominate – the Queen Elizabeth and Argyll Forest Parks – which stretch from the east side of Loch Lomond to Strathyre and across much of the Cowal Peninsula respectively. In addition to timber harvesting, both have been developed for public recreation since the 1950s and now provide many walks, mountain bike trails, wildlife hides and other attractions. There has been a more recent move towards increasing the biodiversity here, with some plantations felled to allow natural regeneration of mixed native woodland.

In parallel with this development has been the surge in public interest and enthusiasm for bird- and wildlife-watching and for botany. All the walks in this guide present the opportunity to spot wildlife and appreciate the changing seasons. Particular highlights include the chance to see feeding ospreys on the lochs and on CCTV at the Lodge Forest Visitor Centre near Aberfoyle. Red squirrels are abundant at Glenbranter and Ardentinny, and if you can visit Inchcailloch Island during late spring, the bluebells are outstanding. The variety of different woodland with the backdrop of freshwater and sea lochs make the autumn a particularly vibrant time to appreciate the tree colours.

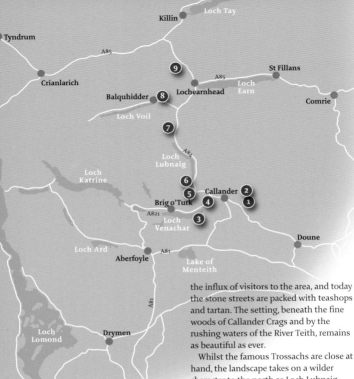

Easily reached from the cities of the central belt, Callander is a true gateway to the Highlands. The first of the Bens, Ben Ledi, overlooks the town, guarding the route north and bringing an abrupt end to the fields and farmland. The publication of *The Lady of the Lake* by Sir Walter Scott began the influx of visitors to the area, and today the stone streets are packed with teashops and tartan. The setting, beneath the fine woods of Callander Crags and by the rushing waters of the River Teith, remains as beautiful as ever.

Whilst the famous Trossachs are close at hand, the landscape takes on a wilder character to the north as Loch Lubnaig extends along the steep-sided glen to the forest village of Strathyre. This is the gateway to the Braes of Balquhidder, the true heart of Rob Roy country and still a remote and lonely cul-de-sac of a glen set beneath the region's highest mountains. Northwards from Strathyre is Lochearnhead, set on the loch of the same name and popular with watersports enthusiasts and fishermen.

Ben Ledi from across Loch Venachar ▶

Callander and Strathyre

Bracklinn Falls

**Distance 5.5km Time 2 hours
Terrain paths with steps, stony tracks and
gated minor road Map OS Landranger 57
Access regular buses from Stirling and
Aberfoyle to Callander**

**A circular walk taking in Bracklinn Falls,
a popular attraction since Victorian times.
The route then follows a forestry track
upstream before crossing the Keltie Water
with views to the remote lands north
of Callander before returning along a
minor road enjoying sweeping views
towards Stirling.**

The car park for Bracklinn Falls is just to
the north of Callander: if walking from the
town centre, head along the main street
towards Stirling and, after the Co-op, take
Bracklinn Road on the left. Follow the signs
as the road leads uphill out of town to

eventually reach the car park on the right.
From here, the walk follows the level path
signed for Bracklinn Falls, passing through
the woods and then an area of open
ground; ignore the track dropping downhill
to the right. Descend some steps to reach
the falls set in a deep ravine a short
distance further on.

The striking wooden bridge replaces a
much earlier cast iron one erected for a visit
by Queen Victoria in around 1870. It was
swept away by a great flood in 2004 which
destroyed eight bridges locally and
inundated houses and shops down in the
town. The new bridge, constructed from
four douglas fir trunks and copper and
weighing 20 tonnes, had to be winched into
position in 2010 because the difficult site is
inaccessible for cranes and helicopters.

Bracklinn is a common name deriving

◀ Bracklinn Falls in full flow

from the Gaelic words *Bhreac*, meaning 'speckled' or 'tawny' (the water is tinged by peat), and *Linn* which means 'pool' or 'waterfall'. The Keltie Water has created the gorge over many hundreds of years, the flow of the water eroding a band of soft puddingstone which lies in a fault at this point and wears away faster than the surrounding rock. Puddingstone is a conglomerate rock made up of many pieces of pebbles and rock held together by quartz sand. The resemblance to the fruit in pudding gives the stone its name.

Cross the bridge and bear left on the path which soon heads into thick pine forest and later climbs fairly steeply through the trees. At a track keep straight ahead and follow this to head north following the Keltie Water (now far below) upstream. Eventually more open ground is reached and there are views to the remote glen of the Keltie Water and the peak of Stuc a'Chroin beyond. Here you get a real sense of being on the boundary between the Highlands and Lowlands.

As the track descends, another waterfall and the deep, still water of Scouts Pool can be seen down to the left. Nowadays it's not just those on Scout camp who brave the

chilly waters and this spot can get popular on hot summer days. When you reach the water cross the bridge and go through the gate to head uphill to the road.

Turn left along this minor road (gated to keep the local livestock in their place) to return towards Callander. Now looking south you get a good view across the flat plain towards Doune and Stirling. The road heads downhill and soon after the next gate turn left to reach the Bracklinn Falls car park at the start.

Callander Crags

Distance 4km **Time** 1 hour 30
Terrain clear paths and forestry tracks,
rocky steps to cairn **Map** OS Landranger 57
Access regular buses from Stirling and
Aberfoyle to Callander

**Climb high above Callander to visit the
Jubilee Cairn and enjoy far-reaching
views over Callander and Stirling in one
direction and over wild and rugged
mountain country in the other. It is
possible to combine this circuit with
nearby Bracklinn Falls.**

This walk can either be approached
from the centre of Callander or from the
Callander Crags car park up the hill.
From Callander, follow the minor road
which heads north from the main street,
signed for Bracklinn Falls and the Golf
Course. At the entrance to the golf course,

continue uphill along the road for
another 300m to reach the car park on the
left. From here, red marker posts show the
way past the information board and
vehicle barrier.

The track weaves its way through mixed
woodland, a haven for birdlife and small
mammals. On reaching a junction,
turn right and climb uphill. Cross a small
bridge, ignoring a path which intersects
the main route, to keep rising uphill with
a couple of wide zigzags. Soon after
passing a picnic bench, the path emerges
into an area of clear ground with another
bench at the top. From here, the line of
crags can be seen straight ahead.

A steep climb with a few rough steps at
the end brings you to the top of the crags.
From the top of the steps, turn right for a
short but slightly awkward detour to the

◀ Beeches on Callander Crags

Jubilee Cairn. Erected in 1897 to celebrate Queen Victoria's Diamond Jubilee, the cairn commands an excellent viewpoint out over Callander, with the Wallace Monument near Stirling clearly visible on a good day – the carseland in this direction is a striking contrast to the empty rolling landscape to the north.

From the cairn, return to the top of the steps and then continue straight ahead to follow the escarpment downhill. The path descends gently through birchwoods at first, with more varied woodland lower down. Ben Ledi is well seen and there are several excellent vantage points for Callander to the left. Further down,

the route crosses a bridge and passes many fine beech trees. Near the bottom of the hill, houses come into view and the path bears left. Ignoring the wide path to the right (which can be used to return to the main street), continue through pleasant woods. Just before a bench, turn left and follow the red marker posts uphill. Turn right at the end of a track for a gentle stroll back to the car park and the start.

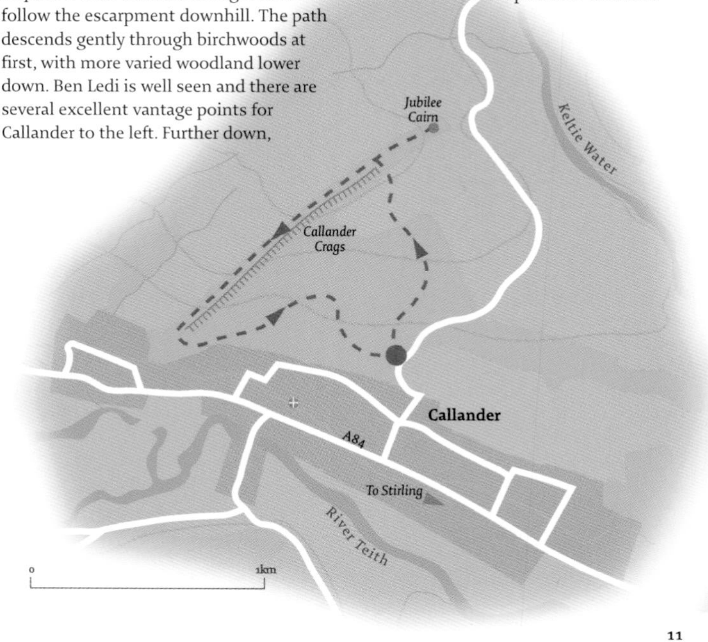

Jubilee
Cairn

Keltie Water

Callander
Crags

Callander

A84

To Stirling

River Teith

0   1km

Loch Venachar and the hidden lochan

Distance 7km **Time** 2 hours
Terrain good forest tracks and surfaced
private roads, suitable for all-terrain
buggies **Map** OS Landranger 57
Access no public transport

The closest of the Trossachs lochs to
Callander is serene Loch Venachar, backed
by the fine outline of Ben Venue when
viewed from its lower end. This walk
discovers a hidden lochan in the forest to
the south of the loch before returning
along the shore.

From the A81 Glasgow/Aberfoyle road in
Callander, branch onto the minor road
which gives access to the Invertrossachs

Estate and leads to the south shore of the
loch. There is a car park on the left just
before the end of the public section of the
road. Walk up the forestry track that begins
here, gradually climbing across the hillside
and soon passing a bench. Continue ahead
when a track joins in from the left to reach
a clear-felled section permitting excellent
views across the loch to the unfamiliar
southern slopes of Ben Ledi.

Tall sitka spruces soon close in and block
out the views once more. At a fork after
1km, turn right to reach Lochan Allt a'Chip
Dhuibh. This secretive sheet of water is so
well hidden by the trees, you won't know
it's there until you're almost upon it;

graceful whooper swans can often be seen gliding along the surface. The track keeps to the north side of the lochan before curving away into the trees. Here you part company with the Rob Roy Way, the unmarked long-distance trail which you have been following from the start.

After passing through a rocky little pass, or bealach in Gaelic, with a small quarry on the right, the route continues with grand views over Loch Venachar ahead. Where it forks, follow the right-hand branch to begin a long and winding descent to the shores of the loch. The white mansion visible over to the left is Invertrossachs

House, visited by Queen Victoria in 1872 during one of her many explorations of the area. The track emerges on a private tarred road, part of National Cycle Network Route 7 which extends from Carlisle to Inverness: turn right along this.

The quiet road gives excellent views across the loch, especially of Ben Ledi opposite and the striking new Harbour Café on the far shore. Continue for 2.5km, passing the Invertrossachs Scout Centre and the sailing club to return to the start.

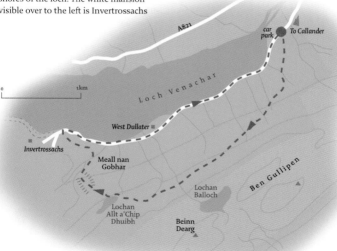

◀ Sunset over Loch Venachar

Bochastle and the Falls of Leny

Distance 7.5km **Time** 2 hours 30
Terrain rough forestry tracks, gentle
climbs, level shared cycle track on disused
railway for return. Suitable for all-terrain
buggies if detour to the falls is omitted
Map OS Landranger 57 **Access** regular
buses from Callander to Kilmahog; walk
past The Lade Inn and over the river to
reach the start

This little-known circuit crosses the flanks
of Bochastle Hill and the lower slopes of
Ben Ledi, with excellent views towards
Loch Lubnaig. The return uses the
cyclepath with a chance to visit the
powerful cataract of the Falls of Leny.

The walk begins from the Bochastle
forestry car park, which is signed from the
A821 just southwest of Kilmahog. Follow
the angled path which rises to meet a
forestry track: turn right onto this. The

best views are back towards Callander
initially, and ahead to Ben Ledi, before
being lost as the track inclines gently into
the dense, dark plantations of sitka spruce.
Further on, this gives way to more
colourful larches. After reaching its highest
point, the track emerges in a felled area.
The next section has a superb outlook
across the glen and down to the foaming
river, but especially ahead to Loch Lubnaig,
enclosed by rugged, steep hills.

Continue along the track until it crosses
a footpath waymarked with blue marker
posts. This is part of the usual ascent route
for Ben Ledi; to continue the circuit, turn
right downhill into the trees. The descent
is very steep in places, but the path is wide
and well-worn. It reaches the road at a
bridge over the river. Don't cross but
instead turn right, following a track into
the Ben Ledi parking area. From here,

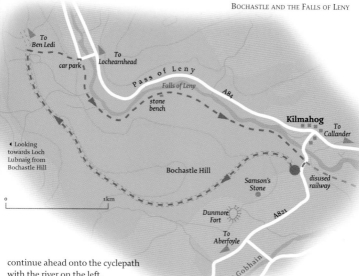

continue ahead onto the cyclepath with the river on the left.

This part of the glen is clothed with very beautiful native oakwoods, threaded by the thundering river – named the Garbh Uisge (Rough Water) for good reason. The cyclepath doesn't visit the Falls of Leny themselves, so to get a closer look turn left onto a rough path at the point where the cyclepath widens and there is a table-like stone. The path is rugged and slippery, and great care is needed when approaching the falls themselves: you'll know you are in the right place as there is a walkway on the opposite side of the river. Though not high, it is the great power of the river that makes the falls so impressive, especially in spate, as the river crashes around a giant central rock.

From here, you can either retrace your steps to carry on along the cyclepath, or alternatively follow the rough path as it makes its way downstream. If choosing the path, keep to the right and follow the higher option at a couple of forks. The oaks are interspersed with fine beech trees as you continue along the glen, now well above the river. Eventually, the path reaches a burn next to a bridge on the cyclepath; here, it is best to join the cycleway as the path beyond becomes very boggy. The cyclepath leads you to the road where, instead of crossing, you turn right and take a path alongside it. This curves right and heads back into Bochastle car park at the start of the walk.

15

Ben Ledi

**Distance 10km Time 5 hours
Terrain steep, rough hill paths;
hillwalking skills and equipment needed.
Best left to mountaineers in snow
Map OS Explorer 365 Access no public
transport to start of walk, nearest bus
stop at Kilmahog**

**Climb the highest mountain in the
Trossachs and be rewarded with
far-reaching views. This route takes the
shortest option up Ben Ledi, although it
is possible to make a more challenging
descent via the Stank Glen for a longer
day out.**

Leave the A84 at the sign for Strathyre
Forest Cabins, cross the bridge and turn
left to reach a parking area: this can
become very busy, so it is best to arrive
early. Start the walk by taking the blue
waymarked path to the left from the
bridge, rising between the pine trees.

After crossing a forestry track, continue
straight ahead for some steep climbing.
The plantations are now left behind as the
route passes through an area newly
planted with native trees. Looking back,
the length of Loch Lubnaig can be seen
below, as well as Callander and the
Lowlands beyond.

The path continues to rise, crossing a
stile at one point and then swinging to the
right to climb up onto the broad southeast
ridge. From here, the path is wet and
eroded in places and crosses two grassy
false summits where, from the second one,
an iron cross comes into view on the
skyline ahead. The cross commemorates
the heroism of Sgt Harry Lawrie, who

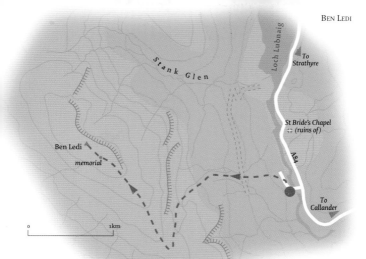

Stank Glen

To Strathyre

Loch Lubnaig

St Bride's Chapel
✝ (ruins of)

A84

Ben Ledi

memorial

To Callander

0   1km

was killed in a tragic accident whilst assisting the Killin Mountain Rescue Team. On 1 February 1987, the rescue team was dealing with an early afternoon call-out to recover the body of a fallen climber near Balquhidder when another call-out was received following reports of a climber having fallen on snowy Ben More. A helicopter, bringing reinforcements for the team, tried to land on the hillside, but its rotor-blade struck a rock causing it to crash. Team member Sgt Lawrie was thrown from the aircraft and killed, whilst other crew members received serious injuries. The rescue team resumed their search the following morning to recover the body of the missing climber.

Just beyond the cross is the cairn and trig point at the summit. As Ben Ledi is the first of the high mountains when approaching

from the south, the views are stunning on a clear day. To the west, Ben Lomond and even the Arrochar Alps on the far side of Loch Lomond can be seen whilst to the north Ben More, Stuc a'Chroin and Ben Lawers are all prominent. To the south is Stirling and the Wallace Monument, whilst the Pentlands are often visible far beyond.

The easiest descent route from the top is to retrace your steps. An alternative descent continues along the northwest ridge and then drops down to the Stank Glen from the bealach. In recent times, the Mountain Rescue Team has been involved in numerous rescues where walkers have missed the correct point at which to descend from the ridge and ended up in difficulties; therefore, the route is only recommended for those confident of their navigational skills.

◀ Approaching the summit of Ben Ledi

Stank Glen

Distance 9km **Time** 3 hours
Terrain tracks, very good paths, some
steep sections **Map** OS Landranger 57
Access no public transport to start of
walk, nearest bus stop at Kilmahog

Explore the upper reaches of the Stank
Glen, a hanging valley, on a picturesque
and hilly circuit. After following Loch
Lubnaig, the route climbs steeply with
great views of the spectacular Stank Burn
waterfalls and more fine views from the
Stank Glen above, then drops back down
the far side of the glen to the loch shore.

The walk starts along an old forest road
just off the A84 north of Callander. Turn
off the main road at the sign for Strathyre
Forest Cabins, crossing the bridge over the
Garbh Uisge and then turning left to
reach a small car park. As this is also the

starting point for Ben Ledi and a popular
section of the Lochs & Glens Route 7 cycle
track, the parking is often all taken so try
to arrive early.

From the car park, return towards the
bridge, but do not cross; instead follow the
lane ahead alongside the river, signed for
Strathyre Forest Cabins. After just over
1km, look out for a sign for Ben Ledi on the
left and join this track as it moves away
from the river and the original lane. From
this point, the route follows red marker
posts. Keep left at a fork in the track and
accompany it on a gentle climb through
woodland. At the sharp corner, keep on the
main track as it zigzags uphill through the
trees. At the third corner, where the track
turns left again, the route diverges uphill
on a path to the right. There is also a short
detour downhill from this corner to view a

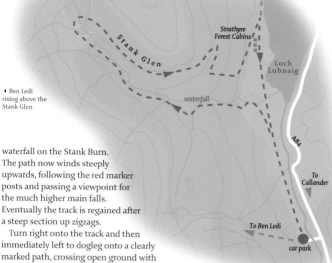

Strathyre Forest Cabins

Stank Glen

Loch Lubnaig

waterfall

A84

◀ Ben Ledi rising above the Stank Glen

To Callander

To Ben Ledi

car park

0   1km

waterfall on the Stank Burn. The path now winds steeply upwards, following the red marker posts and passing a viewpoint for the much higher main falls. Eventually the track is regained after a steep section up zigzags.

Turn right onto the track and then immediately left to dogleg onto a clearly marked path, crossing open ground with good views up the glen. Cross another track to continue on the south side of the glen. This excellent path fords three burns which can usually be achieved without getting your feet wet.

The head of the glen is where walkers bound for the summit of Ben Ledi leave the path. To continue the Stank Glen route, bear right at the junction to head back down the far side of the glen. The path soon becomes a track; turn left at a T-junction to descend gradually. After a corner, you come to another junction. The route swings sharp right here, but it is worth going straight ahead for just a short distance to enjoy a great view over Loch Lubnaig. Once back on the route, continue

downhill following the markers.

Take a path on the left and descend some stone steps, eventually reaching a viewing area for the waterfall seen earlier from the other side of the burn. The path carries on down through birchwoods until it joins a track, bearing left and emerging at the bottom of the glen near the forest cabins. At the junction with the old forestry road, turn right to pass in front of the cabins, with lovely views over Loch Lubnaig. Continue straight ahead and follow the lane along the loch shore and the River Leny all the way back to the start.

19

Beinn an t-Sidhein over Strathyre

Distance 5.5km **Time** 3 hours
Terrain steep ascent; the summit has only
a faint path and is very exposed, so
hillwalking gear is necessary
Map OS Landranger 57 **Access** buses
from Killin and Callander to Strathyre

**A steep ascent of the forested flanks of
the 'Fairy Hill' of Beinn an t-Sidhein
(or Ben Sheann as it's also sometimes
known) to the moorland summit and a
delightful return on an easygoing track
with superb views.**

There is a large car park at the southern
end of Strathyre. Start by stepping up onto
the disused railway line at the back of the
car park and turn left to cross the small
suspension bridge over the River Balvag.
On the far side, bear right up a path which
leads to the back road. Turn right here,
passing the school and keeping an eye on
the left for a signed path which rises up
into the dense trees.

The climb up through the dark forestry
plantation is relentless with only a very
brief respite when you reach a forestry
track. Turn right here for a short dogleg,
before bearing left to continue up a
steep path.

Soon the trees are left behind and

the prominent little peak of Beinn an t-Sidhein is seen for the first time. Ignore the path off to the left and continue uphill. When the path narrows and forks, bear left to cross a small stream and follow a faint path which climbs up through the edge of the fir trees. Once out of the trees look out for another path which heads directly uphill, keeping to the left of a small rocky crag. Follow this rough path to the left of the peak before climbing up from the back to reach the cairn at 546m above sea level. Although the highest summit of Beinn an t-Sidhein is further across the moor to the north, this spot is a far better viewpoint, with Ben Vorlich and Stuc a'Chroin dominant to the east, Ben Lawers rising beyond Lochearnhead to their left and scores of summits to the north and west.

Beinn an t-Sidhein means the 'Fairy Hill' (or knoll) in Gaelic and is a common name for pointed peaks or bumpy ground where fairies and other mythical creatures might dwell. In Gaelic folklore, fairies are often kindly, though sometimes mischievous; however, there are also stories of fairies turning on

their human cohabitants if the humans come too close or attempt to interfere in their ways.

Return back down the path into the woods. On reaching the original forest track turn left and follow this until it meets another track. Head downhill here to reach a minor road. A felled area soon allows great views up the glen.

Bear right here and then left at the next junction to cross a stone bridge over the river. After the bridge, turn right along the old railway line to return to the start.

◀ Loch Lubnaig from Beinn an t-Sidhein

Kirkton Glen and Balquhidder

Distance 9km **Time** 2 hours 30
Terrain good paths and forestry tracks,
with a short steep climb to Creag an Tuirc
Map OS Landranger 51 **Access** buses
from Callander and Killin to Balquhidder

**Visit Rob Roy's grave in the ancient
churchyard at Balquhidder and then
climb to a rocky knoll where a large
cairn signifies this as the rallying point
for the Clan MacLaren. From here, the
MacLaren lands can be surveyed with
good views down to the village and over
Loch Voil. The second part of the walk
follows a traditional route through
more modern forestry in Kirkton Glen to
return to the village.**

Balquhidder is just to the west of the
A84 between Callander and Lochearnhead,
although you have to first turn east and
then pass under the new road to reach it.
Balquhidder's name derives from Gaelic,
meaning 'distant farm' and it is situated at

the start of the 19km-long glen which gets
increasingly wild, ending near the lonely
ruins of a house once belonging to Rob
Roy. Now his grave, which lies next to that
of his wife and sons, is a popular stopping
place. The words 'MacGregor despite them'
carved into the stone represents his
defiance against government efforts to
suppress the unruly clan, including the
banning of the MacGregor name. There is
some parking near the churchyard and
more at the community hall (fee payable).

Start by walking up the lane beside the
churchyard and bear right at the first
junction (SP Kirkton Glen). Very soon, take
a yellow waymarked path rising uphill,
through a gate and eventually reaching the
wooded knoll that is Creag an Tuirc.
Meaning 'Hill of the Boar', this is the
traditional gathering place of the Clan
MacLaren, ancient landowners in this area,
and the spot is marked by the clan cairn.
To warn of impending danger, clan runners

◄ Balquhidder

would be sent up here to sound the clan's rallying cry, which would rouse members to arm themselves and assemble for battle. The strategic importance of this spot is obvious, with sweeping views down over the village, the nearby glens, across Loch Voil and to the mountains beyond.

Retrace a few steps from the summit and then fork right, aiming for a small gate at a track. Turn left to follow this past a bench to a T-junction, where you turn right. At the next two junctions, which come in quick succession, continue straight ahead. Orange markers now show the way towards a group of Scots pine as the track heads up the glen. At a bench, the traditional through-route to Glen Dochart strikes out ahead, but to begin the return to Balquhidder keep to the track turning sharp right and climbing the side of the glen.

The extra height means the views are even better on this section. After 3.5km, the track starts to descend and you turn left at the T-junction to rejoin the original route. When you come to the Kirkton Glen Forestry sign, fork right to wander back through the picturesque village. Turn right at the next turning to cross a footbridge and then an ancient humpback bridge, where you meet the road. Turn left here to return to the start.

Kirkton Burn

Creag an Tuirc Cairn

To Lochearnhead

Balquhidder

Loch Voil

0   1km

Glen Ogle Trail

Distance 4.5km **Time** 4 hours 30
Terrain steep climb up to the railway line;
return route can be very boggy in places
Map OS Landranger 51 **Access** regular
buses from Callander, Killin and Tyndrum
to Lochearnhead

Follow the old railway line out of
Lochearnhead and up towards the pass
on the way to Killin. Before the head
of the pass, the route turns to follow the
old military road back down towards
Loch Earn.

Lochearnhead has an enviable location
overlooking Loch Earn. The loch is unusual
for being subject to a seiche, a tide-like
rise and fall in water level. The casual
visitor is unlikely to notice the effect,
although the prevailing wind that causes
it is much more obvious.

Start from the car park off the A85,
opposite the Watersports Centre. Walk
along the main road back towards the
centre of Lochearnhead, passing the village
hall and crossing the bottom of the Ogle
Burn on the footbridge. At the main
junction, cross the road ahead and turn
right to pass under the old railway line to
St Fillans. Very soon, you turn left up a
track signed for the Scout Station and Glen
Ogle Trail, immediately branching onto a
small path on the right. This rises steeply,
passing through a kissing gate to gain the
old branchline to Killin from the Callander
to Oban railway: it opened in 1886 and ran
until 1965. Although the gradient is gentle,
the long descent meant that the first trains
were restricted to a maximum of 12 miles
per hour so they could negotiate the bends
safely. The planned closure was brought
forward when a landslip in Glen Ogle
blocked part of the line. It is now part of
the National Cycle Network's Lochs and
Glens Route 7 from Carlisle to Inverness.
Turn right to follow it gently uphill,
passing burns and a couple of cattle grids

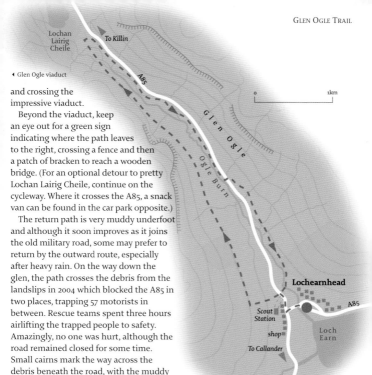

◀ Glen Ogle viaduct

and crossing the impressive viaduct.

Beyond the viaduct, keep an eye out for a green sign indicating where the path leaves to the right, crossing a fence and then a patch of bracken to reach a wooden bridge. (For an optional detour to pretty Lochan Lairig Cheile, continue on the cycleway. Where it crosses the A85, a snack van can be found in the car park opposite.)

The return path is very muddy underfoot and although it soon improves as it joins the old military road, some may prefer to return by the outward route, especially after heavy rain. On the way down the glen, the path crosses the debris from the landslips in 2004 which blocked the A85 in two places, trapping 57 motorists in between. Rescue teams spent three hours airlifting the trapped people to safety. Amazingly, no one was hurt, although the road remained closed for some time. Small cairns mark the way across the debris beneath the road, with the muddy path staying close to the Ogle Burn; further on, a better path winds through the trees alongside the water.

Beyond the second smaller area of landslip debris, the path rises to run parallel to the main road. At a green sign, carefully walk over the road and take the path through grazing land on the far side. After passing over a first stile, climb uphill to another, where an easy burn crossing soon follows and the path carries on down

the glen. Pass through two gates and along the widening path to cross another burn. Go straight ahead through a gate, dropping downhill and over a couple of stiles to enter a wood. Keep on the waymarked path which crosses a bridge over the burn and through the fields to return to the main road. Turn left along it and then left at the next junction to return to the start.

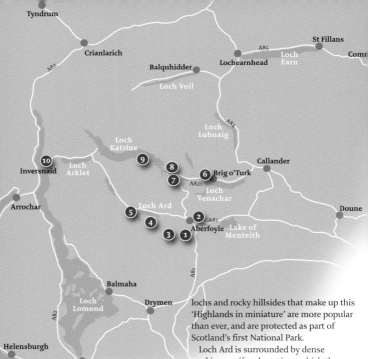

The always-bustling village of Aberfoyle is at the very heart of the Trossachs. Popularised by Sir Walter Scott, this area became immensely fashionable in the 19th century, drawing eminent visitors such as William Wordsworth, John Ruskin and the painter Sir John Everett Millais. Following in their footsteps came thousands on the Victorian 'Grand Tour'. Today the forests, lochs and rocky hillsides that make up this 'Highlands in miniature' are more popular than ever, and are protected as part of Scotland's first National Park.

Loch Ard is surrounded by dense working conifer plantations which the Forestry Commission has worked hard to make attractive to visitors. Loch Venachar has fine sunsets and grand views to Ben Venue. Pretty Loch Achray bathes the feet of the shapely and ever popular little hill of Ben A'an. Pride of place, however, goes to stately Loch Katrine, where the steamship named for Sir Walter Scott still carries thousands of visitors every year across waters that perfectly reflect the stunning woods and hills of this celebrated corner of Scotland.

Autumn on Loch Ard ▶

Aberfoyle and the Trossachs

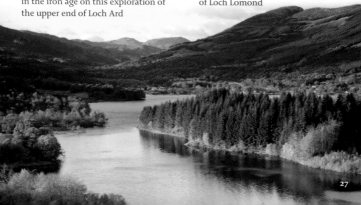

Aberfoyle and Doon Hill

Distance 4.5km **Time** 2 hours
Terrain minor roads, tracks and shared
cyclepath, narrow woodland path;
suitable for buggies, except the detour up
Doon Hill **Map** OS Landranger 57
Access regular buses from Callander
to Aberfoyle

**Visit the fairies of Doon Hill at your peril on
this easy circular walk from Aberfoyle. The
varied route allows you to enjoy this busy
village before exploring the surrounding
open countryside, woodland and riverside,
all with great views.**

There is a large car park just behind the
main street in Aberfoyle, with a tourist
information centre, toilets and the Scottish
Wool Centre – a popular destination in its
own right. Start the walk at the opposite
end of the car park from the Wool Centre

and turn left to cross the stone bridge over
the River Forth.

Follow the road past some houses to
Aberfoyle Cemetery; this is worth a look
around to see the partially restored Kirkton
Church. The graveyard also houses the
tomb of the notorious Reverend Robert
Kirk who was born in Aberfoyle and served
as minister here from 1685 until his
untimely death in 1692. Kirk was a
respected Gaelic scholar, very interested in
local folklore and superstitions. In 1691, he
published a pamphlet entitled *The Secret
Commonwealth Of Elves, Fauns And Fairies*,
describing the secret life of the fairies
who inhabited several hills in the area.
At the time, fairies were the most active
of otherworldly creatures in Highland
mythology and there are numerous stories
about where they lived, what they ate and

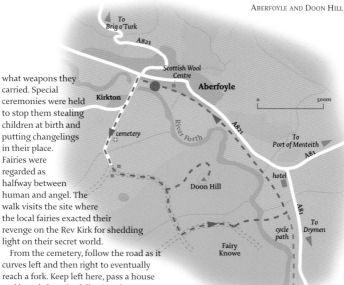

what weapons they carried. Special ceremonies were held to stop them stealing children at birth and putting changelings in their place. Fairies were regarded as halfway between human and angel. The walk visits the site where the local fairies exacted their revenge on the Rev Kirk for shedding light on their secret world.

From the cemetery, follow the road as it curves left and then right to eventually reach a fork. Keep left here, pass a house and keep left again, following the green and red marker posts as the road becomes a rough track. Keep straight ahead, ignoring the two tracks to the left, to pass a green metal gate and gently climb uphill.

Look out for a signpost indicating the detour to the top of Doon Hill. Take this path to the left which winds uphill through the trees until it reaches the tall pine tree at the summit. Legend has it that the fairies kidnapped Revered Kirk and encased his soul in this tree, replacing him with a changeling so that people would believe that the Reverend had died of a heart attack on the hill, allowing his burial in the Kirkton graveyard. It is said that if you circle the tree seven times you will be bestowed with good luck. Many people

have left clooties (rags) and other offerings that festoon the branches.

Return the same way down to the track, turning left to continue the circuit. Cross a bridge and turn left at the next junction. Take care as these tracks are used by cyclists and sometimes the local husky dog sled teams racing at high speed. There are good views to Doon Hill. At the next junction turn left, following the sign for Aberfoyle, crossing a small bridge and heading between fields. At the T-junction, turn left over a small bridge to join the old railway line, now a cycletrack, which leads back to Aberfoyle, emerging at the car park near the Wool Centre.

◀ The old kirkyard

The Lime Craig Circuit

Distance 6km **Time** 2 hours
Terrain waymarked trail on good paths,
steep sections **Map** OS Landranger 57
Access regular buses from Callander to
Aberfoyle; there is a steep 500m walk to
the visitor centre from the west end
of Aberfoyle

Follow the Highland Boundary Fault
which divides the Highlands from the
Lowlands on this waymarked trail from
just outside Aberfoyle. Watch for red
squirrels and ospreys, but keep an even
closer eye out for the bizarre sight of
humans flying above the canopy
of trees.

The walk starts high above Aberfoyle at
the Lodge Forest Visitor Centre, the main

Forestry Commission visitor centre for the
area (parking fee). Facilities include live
CCTV footage of nesting ospreys in the
spring and summer months, as well as a
café with spectacular terrace views. Several
walks begin here: this route follows the red
marker posts and starts from the right side
of the building as you face it and heads
along the top of the high ground to pass a
statue of a lumberjill, one of many women
who served in the Timber Corps during
both world wars. The path doubles back to
descend into the glen below.

Keep straight on until you reach a
junction with a bronze deer sculpture; turn
left here and soon cross a wooden
boardwalk over a marshy area. Keep right at
the junctions until the trail descends once
more into a peaceful and pretty wooded

dell: to the left, a burn drops in an impressive double waterfall.

Go across the footbridge signed for National Cycle Network Route 7, picking up the track which bears left, with red marker posts once more. Further on, a secretive boardwalk path to the right offers the chance to visit a hide to view small birds and red squirrels at the well-stocked feeders. Continuing on the track, turn left at a junction to begin a long but steady climb. Overhead is the network of rope bridges, zipwires and climbing nets that make up the assault course, usually occupied by fearless children followed by terrified parents. Soon you come to a bench and waterfall just off to the left, giving a chance for a break as the main track carries on uphill.

At a crossroads, turn right and carry on to reach Lime Craig. Situated on the natural fault that divides the mountainous Highlands from the flatter Lowlands, this was once the site of a lime quarry. Here, it is possible to add a strenuous short excursion to the top of the crag for superb views. To do this, follow the sign for the viewpoint, climbing steeply across the slope to the left at first, passing between gateposts and turning right up the track to the top. The panorama includes Aberfoyle far below, with the fertile plains stretching away to the Campsies and Fintry Hills on one side, and the mountains of the Trossachs on the other. Return to the main trail at Lime Craig and accompany the path as it drops steeply through the woods, with good views of Aberfoyle on the way. The path follows the straight line of an old wagonway built in the 1800s to ferry the limestone from the quarry to the kilns below. The lime was smelted to produce lime mortar and other building products as well as fertiliser. Go straight across a track part way down the slope. At the bottom, turn right to follow another forestry track, then left onto a path. Cross a footbridge and turn right at a signed junction. Continue ahead as the red markers guide you up a series of zigzags to the visitor centre.

◂ Woodland surrounding the Lodge Forest Visitor Centre

Lochan Spling

Distance 6km Time 2 hours
Terrain waymarked forestry tracks, suitable
for all-terrain buggies – except viewpoint
Map OS Landranger 57 Access regular buses
from Callander to Aberfoyle

This waymarked forestry walk leads to an
attractive forest loch with the unusual
name of Lochan Spling. An easy excursion
from Aberfoyle, the route takes in several
sculptures with riddles for families, the
chance to get your bearings at a viewpoint
and superb autumn colour.

Start from the riverside car park in
Aberfoyle and make for the road at the
western end. Turn left and cross the stone
humpback bridge over the River Forth.
Carry on along Manse Road before taking
the third turning on the right uphill
(Duchray Road).

Soon Inchrie Castle is passed: also
known later as the Covenanters' Inn, it was
built as a private home in the 1800s in the
Italianate style, looking slightly ill at ease
among the Highland trees and mountains.
The name comes from a meeting held here
in 1949 when the Second Covenant calling
for a separate Scottish parliament was
issued by the Scottish Covenant
Association. Two million people signed
the covenant in the next few years, but
Scotland did not regain a parliament until
1997. The Inn has another place in
nationalist folklore: when the Stone of
Scone, also known as the Stone of Destiny,
was stolen from Westminster Abbey in
1950 (by members of the Scottish
Covenant Association), some say it was
temporarily hidden here in a basement.

Continue along the road past a fine arts

◀ Lochan Spling

and crafts-style house and onto the rougher forest track. At a junction, turn right, signed for Milton Car Park. At the bottom of the small hill, as the track bends to the left, a path heads straight ahead uphill for an optional detour to a viewpoint high above Lochan Spling before looping back to the track further on. If ignoring the detour, the track leads to the loch shore where there is a metal sculpture of a pike and a great view of Ben Lomond in the distance.

Follow the track alongside the water as it passes a dragonfly sculpture and reunites with the path from the viewpoint. The track turns away from the loch and eventually reaches a T-junction. Here, turn left, signed for Kinlochard, to soon reach the final sculpture: an osprey, a bird which often feeds in this area. An osprey eyrie can be viewed via CCTV at the Lodge Forest Visitor Centre just north of Aberfoyle.

At the next junction, the route turns left onto another track. There are glimpses of Lochan Spling through the trees to the left, and soon the outward route is rejoined at a crossroads. Keep straight on, passing Inchrie Castle and turning left to cross the stone bridge into Aberfoyle.

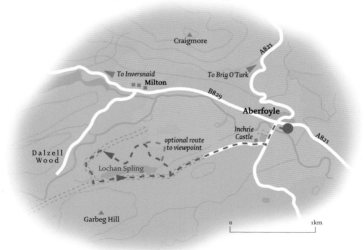

Loch Ard and Lochan Ghleannain

Distance 6.75km Time 2 hours
Terrain good, waymarked forestry tracks
suitable for all-terrain buggies; short
optional section on rougher woodland
path Map OS Landranger 57 Access regular
buses from Aberfoyle: alight at Milton and
walk up the track to Loch Ard car park. It is
possible to walk from Aberfoyle via
Lochan Spling, adding 3km and 1 hour
each way (see p32)

This excellent easygoing forestry trail
passes a picturesque lochan before
visiting the quiet side of Loch Ard. With
sculptures to view along the way, it makes
for an ideal family outing.

Start from the Loch Ard Forestry car park
at Milton, off the B829 to the west of
Aberfoyle. (To approach from Aberfoyle on

foot, take the Lochan Spling walk as far
as the T-junction after the dragonfly:
turn right and follow signs for the
Milton car park, taking a path on the left
to the start.)

Cross the entrance track for the car park
and take the track straight in front,
indicated by red posts. Bear right when it
forks and carry on to Lochan Ghleannain,
with its flowering waterlilies in summer.
The track runs along the water's edge
before gaining height.

Keep to the track and follow the yellow
waymarkers as you pass through mixed
woodland and begin heading downhill.
At the bottom, Loch Ard comes into view.
Here, you'll find a picnic table and, in the
trees, an amusing sculpture showing
native red squirrels battling with invading

◄ A window on Loch Ard

greys. Turn right along the wider track here. At the next junction look left to join a loop path which keeps closer to the loch, which is well-stocked with brown trout and popular with anglers, as well as being the focal point for 26km of waymarked footpaths and cycle trails. This path is rougher and can be avoided by staying on the main track, but it does give lovely views across the water to the grand houses on the far shore. Keep on the clear path through the trees, staying left when you see a branch to the right.

The path passes above a cave in the cliff, said to have been used as a hiding place by Rob Roy, but it is only visible and accessible by boat.

When the path rejoins the main track, turn left and look out for a series of sculptures hidden in the trees on this stretch. A large wooden acorn and an eagle are easy to spot, but a skulk of foxes are, appropriately, more elusive. The track eventually reaches two houses which you pass on the left. Soon after, turn right to return to the car park at the start.

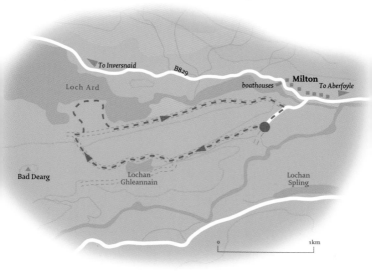

Kinlochard and the crannog

Distance 10.5km **Time** 3 hours 30
Terrain tracks and paths with one steep
section; suitable for all-terrain buggies as
far as the crannog **Map** OS Landranger 57
Access no public transport to start

Step out into true Rob Roy country,
exploring the lochside and farmland of
MacGregor territory on this easy going
circuit. After passing the ancient remains
of Loch Ard's iron age crannog, the route
climbs briefly to return along a forestry
track with superb views across the water
to distant Ben Lomond and a good chance
of spotting deer and birds of prey.

The walk begins at the small forestry
village of Kinlochard at the western end of

Loch Ard. The car park is up a track on the
right just after Lochard Cottages. From
here, return to the road and turn right to
follow it towards the buildings of
Blairhullichan and Couligartan. Pass the
entrance to the sailing club and continue
on the now private road with good views
down over Loch Ard. Described by Sir
Walter Scott in his novel *Rob Roy* as 'an
enchanting sheet of water', Loch Ard is
often regarded as the jewel in the crown of
the Trossachs lochs.

Where a track heads down to the left, go
straight on, passing to the right of the
houses. Continue for 150m past a small
iron-clad house before turning left at a
junction. The narrow track passes through

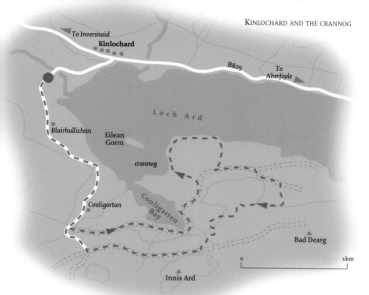

dense rhododendrons as well as native trees before reaching more open ground and finally the shore at the deep bay.

At the next junction, take the left turning, signed for the crannog. Just before you reach the water, go right and from here it is possible to head down to the shore for a better view of the crannog, visible just to the left of the much larger Eliean Gorm. Crannogs were iron age roundhouses built on small artificial islands in the water, either for defence or simply as a status symbol. Follow the track above the shoreline, passing a seat with a lovely view as the route turns towards the eastern end of Loch Ard.

At a T-junction, bear left (heading right here is a shortcut back to the start).

The track climbs gently uphill, passing a turning to the left and branching right at the next signed junction. After passing a felled area, the path narrows and rises steeply uphill.

Where the path levels off, a bench gives walkers the chance to relax and enjoy a truly superb view over Loch Ard, especially stunning when seen in the autumn. The distinctive outline of Ben Lomond, visible to the left, completes the picture. From the bench, turn right along a level track. Immediately after a vehicle barrier, turn right. Keep right at the next fork, continuing downhill. This soon rejoins the outward route; go straight ahead to follow the private road back to Kinlochard.

The Brig o'Turk loop

Distance 5.5km **Time** 2 hours
Terrain waymarked paths, some ascent,
minor roads **Map** OS Landranger 57
Access no public transport to start

Brig o'Turk was a staging post on the
Grand Tour in the heart of the Trossachs.
Surrounded by beautiful scenery, it was
visited by Queen Victoria and Prince
Albert on their extensive travels in the
Highlands. It was also celebrated by
poets and painters, with Millais, Ruskin
and Wordsworth all staying in the village.

At the time of Queen Victoria's visit, the
landlady at the inn was known as Muckle
Kate on account of her ample waistline and
formidable features. She was said to always
wear a large apron into which she would
deposit the takings and often 'forget' to
extract customers' change, preferring to see
if they would challenge her for it. Queen
Victoria presented her with a gold
sovereign, but it is not reported if she was

expecting change. The village today is still
small with an inn, a tearoom famous for its
part in the 1958 film version of the 39 *Steps*,
starring Kenneth More, a scattering of
houses, village hall and school.

The walk starts from the Little Drum
Wood car park to the east of Brig o'Turk on
the south side of the A821, opposite the
driveway for Lendrick Lodge. Follow the
path next to the information board. When
you reach a gate, don't go through it,
instead keeping left on the waymarked
path which climbs through the woods.
After passing a bench, ignore the pink
waymarked route to the right for now and
instead turn left at the next junction, soon
reaching a viewpoint.

The path bends sharply right to meander
through the trees. At a T-junction, turn left
to head down through an iron gate and
detour to the shore of Loch Venachar, an
attractive reservoir popular with anglers
and hunting ospreys.

◀ Shore of Loch Venachar

Go back up the wide path, carrying straight on at the junction until you return to the start of the pink waymarked trail passed earlier. This time, turn left to follow it as it inclines up to run along a rocky crag before crossing more open ground with a view of Ben Venue ahead. Keep a sharp eye out for the markers as the path is faint and muddy in places. At a boulder, turn right, dropping to the main road and crossing it to pass through a gate on the far side. Keep your feet dry on the boardwalk above the boggy ground which was once the village curling pond.

Follow the path through the birchwoods, turning right at a junction to reach a minor road. Head straight across this and take the path running beside the River Finglas. Before the gate, turn left (SP Village), soon joining the road past the houses. You can

detour up the road beside the tearoom to reach the bicycle tree, also known locally as the metal-eating tree. A large sycamore, it stands near the side of an old smiddy and legend has it that bits of old iron propped up against it were slowly devoured by the growing tree. A pair of protruding handlebars are the only reminder of an old bicycle, apparently left leaning against the tree when its young owner went off to the First World War, never to return.

Continue along the main road to the edge of the village. When the pavement runs out, carry on along a footpath and then go through a gate on the right-hand side of the road into fields. This soon rejoins the outward path: follow this, keeping straight ahead to reach the junction in the woods near the start. Turn left here for the car park.

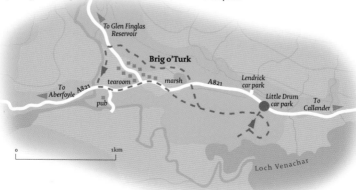

Achray Water bridge circuit

Distance **4.5km** Time **1 hour 30**
Terrain **path, forest track and minor road**
Map **OS Landranger 57** Access **no public transport to start**

Loch Achray nestles below steep wooded hillsides, perfectly reflected on its surface on still days. The name 'Trossachs' actually refers to the steep and rugged glen between the foot of Loch Katrine and Loch Achray and it is only in recent times that it has come to apply to the wider region. This route explores the original Trossachs, following the course of the Achray Water and perhaps whetting your appetite for a climb up one of the nearby mountains.

Start from the Ben Venue car park (parking fee), just south of the turning for Loch Katrine on the A821. Take the path near the information board opposite the car park entrance, initially marked by blue posts. (This is the same path for Ben Venue, a 725m-high mountain which is a popular objective.) The waters of Loch Achray can be seen from this section and also the distinctive summit of Ben A'an, shaped like a thimble from this direction. At the path junction leave the blue waymarkers and turn right.

Cross a wooden boardwalk which leads across the marsh to reach a minor road. Turn left along the road (this eventually leads to the dam at Loch Katrine). Ben Venue can be seen straight ahead in clear weather as you make your way alongside the sometimes-bubbling torrent of Achray Water. As its flow is controlled by the dam and used as part of the hydro-

◀ Ben Venue rising above the woods

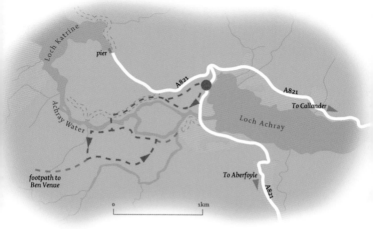

electric scheme, the water level and speed can change very rapidly. Well before reaching Loch Katrine, and before the road bends, look out for a path off to the left for Ben Venue. This leads you over the Achray Water by a wooden humpback bridge, beyond which you continue to a track. Take the right-hand option here, signposted for Ben Venue. After a few hundred metres, turn left onto another path for a climb through trees. This path winds its way through the woods before descending to join another track. At this point, the route to Ben Venue goes off to the right. A full day is required to climb this peak, as well as a map, compass and hillwalking gear and skills (the route is very boggy in parts and rocky higher up), so instead turn left.

As the track drops gently downhill, Ben A'an is seen once more across the forest. When climbing Ben A'an, it looks and feels like a totally separate peak; however, from this angle it is clear that it is really only a shoulder of the higher, rolling hill behind. At a crossroads, continue straight ahead and accompany the track to a T-junction by the Achray Water. Turn left here (signed for Ben Venue car park) and continue to the junction met earlier in the walk. Take the right turn for the path back over the Achray Water bridge. On the far side, turn right along the private road to retrace your steps, turning right onto the boardwalk path just before the public road. To return to the car park, turn right after the boardwalk and follow the blue waymarkers back.

Ben A'an

Distance 3.7km **Time** 4 hours
Terrain rocky and steep path, a good
'mountain' expedition for older children
if care is taken **Map** OS Landranger 57
Access no public transport to start

Ben A'an is one of the best-loved and
most prominent peaks in the Trossachs.
Although at 461m high, it is really just a
rocky shoulder of the higher moorland
beyond, its fantastic views and dominant
position at the heart of the Trossachs
make it an ideal objective for those
looking to attain a summit with the
feel of a real mountain top.

Start from the Ben A'an car park (parking
charge) on the south side of the A821
near Loch Achray. The actual walk begins
on the other side of the road, where a
wide signed path climbs uphill before
following a burn.

Cross a wooden footbridge and keep on
climbing until a rocky knoll to the left of
the path is reached. Here, a bench is well
sited to enjoy the lovely view back down to
Loch Achray. As the path continues the
dramatic pointed summit of Ben A'an
appears ahead for the first time. At this
stage, some walkers have been known to
admit defeat and head back; however, the

actual route is not as demanding as it looks from this angle, as it sweeps round to reach the summit from behind – though undoubtedly the ascent is still steep.

There is a beautiful section of birchwood before the path aims for the gap to the right of the seemingly unassailable summit pyramid. Ignore the apparent shortcuts and keep to the main path as it climbs around the rocky back of the summit before swinging to the left. There are great views up beautiful Loch Katrine,

where the steamer can often be seen making its serene progress. One final rocky section leads to the summit itself which has commanding views over the whole of the Trossachs, including almost the entire length of Loch Katrine as well as Loch Achray and a large part of Loch Venachar. To the west, Ben Lomond is the prominent pointed summit on the skyline, whilst Ben Venue looks extremely impressive across the narrow foot of Loch Katrine. The return is by the same outward route.

Loch Katrine

pier

Ben A'an

hotel

To Callander

A821

Loch Achray

A821

To Aberfoyle

0   1km

Loch Katrine

Distance 21km **Time** 5 hours
Terrain private tarmac road throughout,
giving easy walking despite the length,
suitable for buggies **Maps** OS Landranger
56 and 57 **Access** no public transport
to start. It is always a good idea to book
the steamship in advance

This long but easy walk is a fantastic way
to appreciate the wild setting and beauty
of Loch Katrine. First, take a morning ride
on the steamship, the *SS Sir Walter Scott*,
from Trossachs Pier to the start point at
Stronachlachar, and then follow the
private road around the loch to return.

The summertime steamer alights at
Stronachlachar Pier late in the morning,
leaving plenty of time for the return walk.
From the tearoom, walk up the road and
turn right after Hillview Cottage. Pass a
white gate and follow the road towards the
water's edge, passing the backs of some

fine houses. Once the cyclists from the boat
have gone past, the road is very quiet.
Owned by Scottish Water, it dates to when
the reservoir was created to supply water to
Glasgow. The scheme was opened by
Queen Victoria in 1859 and reportedly sales
of soap fell by a half in parts of Glasgow as
the clean, soft water made an easy lather.

At the slipway, Factors Isle can be seen
straight ahead. Here, Rob Roy MacGregor
imprisoned a rent collector in revenge for
the eviction of his family from their lands.
The water level has been raised several
times and the island is now protected by an
ornamental wall. After the vehicle barrier,
keep to the road as it winds through open
countryside with glorious views.

Near the head of the loch, Glengyle
House can be seen on the far side, the
birthplace of Rob Roy.

The road curves around on a new bridge
at the head of the loch to reach the house,

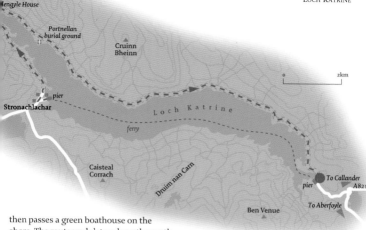

then passes a green boathouse on the shore. The route undulates along the north side of the loch through pines and, later, woods of oak, birch and beech. Any climbs are brief and amply rewarded with glimpses of the water or tumbling waterfalls as the road crosses a number of small burns.

After passing the house at Portnellan, the burial ground of Clan MacGregor can be seen jutting out into the loch. This is well worth the short detour; the graves date from 1699 to 1800 and are guarded by an impressive wall and gate, a lovely place for a rest. The route now winds along the side of the loch, passing in and out of woodland. It dips to cross a burn by the site of an old schoolhouse. This is a reminder of a time when the glen supported hundreds of families. Keep following the track through the tiny settlements of Strone, Edra and Letters, passing a pier and boathouse.

The final part of the walk is the most beautiful of all, with small islands guarding

the entrance to Trossachs Pier. It is possible to gauge how close you are to the end of the walk by the number of wobbly cyclists and golf buggies, both of which can be hired at the pier. The Trossachs became hugely popular as a tourist destination in the 19th century after the publication of *The Lady of the Lake* and *Rob Roy* by Sir Walter Scott. Initially, a rowing boat crewed by eight ferried passengers up the loch. A steamship began in competition and the rowers spent a week racing with their new rival. At the end of the week, the steamship was found sunk in its mooring. The rowers were brought to court but refused to cooperate, speaking only Gaelic and claiming that a mythical creature, a Water Horse, had submerged the vessel. The case was dismissed due to a lack of evidence, but soon the current steamship, the *SS Sir Walter Scott*, took their place and continues to this day.

◀ The SS Sir Walter Scott

Inversnaid RSPB Trail

**Distance 2.5km Time 1 hour
Terrain waymarked, narrow and hilly
woodland path Map OS Landranger 56
Access Inversnaid Explorer from Tarbet
pier (June-Sept), or ferry run by
Inversnaid Hotel from Inveruglas, west
Loch Lomondside**

**This short but steep little nature trail
explores the oakwoods on the east
side of Loch Lomond, beginning at
Inversnaid, celebrated in poetry by
Gerard Manley Hopkins.**

The walk begins at the large hotel at
Inversnaid on the east side of Loch
Lomond. It can be reached either via a very
long and winding road from Aberfoyle in
the Trossachs, or alternatively by taking a

ferry from Inveruglas or Tarbet on the west
side of the loch. Inversnaid was a halt on
the Grand Tour during the 19th century;
well-heeled tourists would approach by
boat before being taken from Inversnaid by
horse and coach to Stronachlachar, where
they would sail on down Loch Katrine.
Today, the hotel here is the base for coach
holidays, but it still enjoys a peaceful and
very beautiful spot.

The walk begins by following the West
Highland Way north from the large car
park. A sign soon indicates the start of the
Inversnaid Nature Reserve, owned and
maintained by the RSPB. Beautiful
oakwoods sweep down from the hills to
the shore of the loch, packed with native
birch, rowan, hazel and holly as well as

◀ Inversnaid Hotel from across Loch Lomond

oak. Continue along the West Highland Way, passing behind an old corrugated iron boathouse. Pipelines can be seen running steeply down the flanks of Ben Vorlich on the opposite side of the loch to feed the hydro-electric power station at Inveruglas.

Just before a little wooden bridge, a sign indicates the start of the nature trail, joined by turning right uphill into the woods. The climb is steep but very enjoyable, with the ruins of the old settlement of Cladachbeag scattered beneath the canopy of trees. Eventually the path emerges at a clearing with a bench and a fine view back down the length of Loch Lomond, peppered with islands. Opposite, towering above Tarbet, are the mountains of the Arrochar Alps.

The path now begins to descend back through the woods, crossing a wooden footbridge over a burn. Once back at the loch shore, you meet the West Highland Way again. A glance at the map shows a tempting detour to the right to visit Rob Roy's cave; however, this old hide-out of the noble rogue really only consists of a cleft amongst broken rocks and isn't worth the awkward clamber needed to reach it. Instead, turn left to return to Inversnaid along the beautiful path beside the loch.

The poet Gerard Manley Hopkins stayed at Inversnaid, and the lines he wrote here are often quoted by conservationists and wild nature enthusiasts:

What would the world be, once bereft
Of wet and wildness? Let them be left,
Oh let them be left, wildness and wet;
Long live the weeds and wilderness yet.

Britain's largest body of freshwater, Loch Lomond, is justly famous and must rank amongst the most beautiful lochs in Scotland. Immortalised by romantic ballads, and just a short hop from Glasgow, it draws visitors by the thousand, but still nothing detracts from the sheer majesty of the loch, sprinkled with the greenest of islands, fringed with the finest of woodland and backed by the silhouette of Ben Lomond.

Balloch, on the southern shore, is almost a suburb of Glasgow and home to a giant upmarket retail development and visitor hub right on the edge of the loch. Nearby, the lovely Balloch Castle Country Park offers a great venue for family rambles and picnics. The east side of the loch is spared the thundering traffic of the A82 to the west, and the landscape becomes progressively grander and more beautiful the further one goes. Balmaha, on the very boundary of the Highlands, is a jumping-off point for boating trips to the islands. From here, the famous West Highland Way weaves a course through ancient oakwoods to Rowardennan and the very end of the road. Here begins the ascent of mighty Ben Lomond with its unparalleled views.

Loch Lomond East

Balloch Castle Country Park

Distance 3.5km Time 1 hour
Terrain excellent paths, suitable for
buggies Map OS Landranger 56
Access Balloch is well served by buses and
trains: it is a 500m walk from the station
and centre to South Lodge

Explore a 200-acre country park at the
southern end of Loch Lomond with
mature woodland and beautiful views
over the water. A great place for all the
family, with a children's play area, toilets,
refreshments and horticultural interest at
the lovely walled garden.

There is a large car park near the castle,
but if starting from the bus stop on Balloch
Road or from Balloch itself, turn into the
park at the South Lodge and walk along the
South Drive until you reach the car park.
From the far end of the car park, follow the
waymarked path past a couple of enormous
pine trees to a junction. Turn right here,

looking out for the final resting place of
Bran, a dog who once lived at the castle.
Carry on along the tarmac path which runs
between an avenue of rhododendrons and
large trees, with fine views over Loch
Lomond below.

These landscaped grounds were laid out
after the present-day castle was built in
1808. Strongly influenced by Capability
Brown, they were designed by Robert
Lugar. The castle was built partly from the
wealth generated by Glasgow's first bank,
the Ship Bank established in 1749, which
later became embroiled in a banking war
between the older established banks based
in Edinburgh and the new upstarts in
Glasgow. The Edinburgh banks tried to
gather in all their own-issued banknotes in
order to force a credit crisis and bankrupt
the Glaswegians. However, the Ship Bank
survived and John Buchanan, a Tory MP
and partner in the bank, had Balloch Castle

◀ Seat with a view, Balloch Castle Country Park

built in the Scottish Baronial style with turrets and castellated walls, using some of the bank's profits.

The path soon enters Horsehouse Wood, curving round the far end of the park to loop back near the loch shore. The clean air here was seen as a tonic for the people of Glasgow, many of whom lived in overcrowded, insanitary conditions and, in 1915, the City Council bought the park for the recreational benefit of its residents. Ahead, the last paddle steamer built in Britain, the *Maid of the Loch*, comes into view at the foot of the loch. She is being restored so that she can again take passengers onto the water under steam. The path passes a slipway and a large children's play area to the left.

Follow the path slightly uphill, passing the scant remains of the original castle. Plundered for its stone when the current mansion was built, only the faint shape of the moat and mound remains. It was built in the early 13th century by the Earl of Lennox and remained the family stronghold until around 1390 when the family switched to Inchmurrin Island. The Lennox family provided a rich supply of Scottish nobles and royalty, including Lord

Darnley, the King Consort of Mary Queen of Scots, who was murdered at Kirk o' Field in Edinburgh in 1567.

The path runs beside the River Leven, passing many moored boats. Keep on the surfaced route as it bears left and is lined with streetlights. Follow white pebbles to the left to explore the walled garden. Once the kitchen garden for the castle, it had fallen into neglect until its restoration in 2002. Leave the garden by the same archway and turn left to accompany orange markers to rejoin the main path. Turn left onto the tarmac drive and left at a fork to the back of Balloch Castle. Detour to the front of the building to admire the architecture and vantage point over the loch. Return to the rear of the building and take the road back to the car park.

Duncryne Hill by Gartocharn

Distance 1.25km **Time** 45 mins
(add 45 mins for round-trip from
Gartocharn) **Terrain** narrow but good
path through bracken, steady climb
Map OS Landranger 56 **Access** regular
buses from Alexandria and Balloch or
from Balfron to Gartocharn

Follow in the footsteps of the late and
much-loved outdoors broadcaster Tom
Weir on this short ramble. He reckoned
that the view from the top of this small
hill was the best in the district, with Loch
Lomond and its islands backed by the
great peaks of the Southern Highlands.

This walk can be started either from the
village of Gartocharn or from a parking
area adjacent to the woods below
Duncryne Hill itself. Walking from
Gartocharn along the pleasant country
road adds approximately 1.5km to the
round trip. Leave Gartocharn by the minor
road heading south towards Duncryne,
whose prominent shape can be seen across
the fields to the left. Soon the road runs
alongside a wood and there is a layby
parking area – the alternative start point.

From the far end of the wood, take the
signed path through the gate on the left
into the trees. This native woodland is a

haven for birdlife. Go through a kissing gate at the other end and ahead through another gate onto a grassy lane (often wet underfoot) leading through the fields to the foot of Duncryne. The hill is, in fact, the hardened remains of a volcano – a volcanic plug of which there are many examples in Scotland, including the hill upon which Edinburgh Castle sits. At Duncryne, the perfectly round dome shape has led to its being known by locals as the Dumpling. At only 142m (460 feet) above sea level, its height is probably only worthy of a pudding, but the fact that it rises starkly from the flat lands around and has dramatic views up the length of Loch Lomond has elevated its status.

A second kissing gate leads into a small section of woodland at the base of the hill. Follow the path which bears right and then, once out of the woods, starts to ascend the bracken-covered slope to the bare summit. Here, a large trig point marks the summit and makes a perfect back-rest to enjoy the view.

On a clear day, Loch Lomond is spread out below, dotted with beautiful wooded islands. For the backdrop, there is a superb panorama of mountains including favourite summits such as The Cobbler, Ben Vorlich and, dominant, Ben Lomond. Tom Weir, the legendary bobble-hatted climber and walker, best known for presenting *Weir's Way* on TV, lived in Gartocharn and for many years made this ascent daily.

Being such a small hill, there is no alternative route down and, therefore, the return is by the same outward path.

◀ View from the Dumpling

Conic Hill from Balmaha

Distance 5.25km **Time** 3 hours 30
Terrain steep climb on grassy path,
avoidable rocky scramble near top
Map OS Landranger 56 **Access** regular
buses from Balloch to Balmaha

Conic Hill is a moderate hill walk with
views that rival even mighty Ben
Lomond. From the top, it is possible to
pick out the jagged ridges of the
mountains on Arran, as well as the
distinctive shape of Ailsa Craig off the
Ayrshire coast, but it is the view over
Loch Lomond and the line of islands that
follow the Highland Boundary Fault that
put this hill at the top of the list.

Start from the car park in the centre of
Balmaha and take the path from the far
end by the information board, turning

right at the T-junction onto a track and
then left onto a path. This section follows
part of the long-distance trail, the West
Highland Way, which is marked with the
distinctive thistle symbol. The route
climbs through the trees, passing through
a gate to emerge onto open ground.

Keep on the path as it rises more steeply,
ascending sets of wooden steps as it aims
for a low point between Conic Hill and the
nearer slopes on the left. Pass through this
gap to reach a West Highland Way marker:
from here the route bears right to run
across the far side of Conic Hill, with
excellent views over Loch Lomond and the
mountains beyond.

Continue along the West Highland Way
until you're almost at its highest point,
where a clear path branches right to gain

the ridge; the summit is then a short distance to the left. The ridge, which has awkward rockier sections if joined too soon, is right on the line of the Highland Boundary Fault. Look across Loch Lomond and you will see a string of islands in a perfect line, marking this geological feature, once the cause of frequent earthquakes. The rocks underfoot are ancient, derived from the Himalayan-scale mountains which once stood to the northwest side of the fault. As the hills eroded, some of the loosened rocks fused to form a conglomerate known as puddingstone for its obvious resemblance to fruit pudding.

To begin the descent, retrace your steps to rejoin the West Highland Way. Turn left to reach the marker post passed earlier in the walk. Now there is a choice of return routes. The easiest is to continue along the outward route, whilst the alternative is much rougher and steeper but gives superb views. To make this rough descent, carry on down the grassy ridge from the marker post. After a while, cut across to the right to join another ridge which has fabulous views every step of the way, looking over the loch and its islands

directly ahead. The last section down to the road is very steep, however, the path being rough and badly eroded in places, so care is needed.

Cross the road and head slightly to the left to take a path across the field opposite: this soon comes to the edge of Loch Lomond and rejoins the West Highland Way. Turn left, staying on the waterside path when the West Highland Way veers off to the left. The path, which has been hewn from the rocky shores, takes you to a bridge and the end of a lane. Follow this surfaced road to the centre of Balmaha.

◀ Hairy coo on Conic Hill

Inchcailloch Island

Distance 3km **Time** 1 hour 30
Terrain clear paths with some gentle
ascent; steps from the boat and in the
woodland make it unsuitable for buggies
Map OS Landranger 56 **Access** regular
buses from Balloch to Balmaha; boat
from Balmaha Boatyard to Inchcailloch

**Cross the water from Balmaha to visit
this beautiful wooded isle. A network of
paths leads you around sites where kings
once hunted deer, an Irish princess lived
in a religious order and locals came to
bury their dead. Today the island is a
nature reserve and a wonderful spot to
watch wildlife against the backdrop of
Loch Lomond.**

Inchcailloch, one of a string of islands
dotted about in the southern end of Loch
Lomond, has drawn visitors and longer-
term inhabitants for thousands of years.

One of the first Irish saints to come to
Scotland to spread christianity was
Kentigerna, who lived on the island more
or less as a hermit following the death of
her husband, a king of the Gaelic kingdom
of Dalriada. Kentigerna, the mother of
Saint Fillan, established a small nunnery
on the island and died here in 734AD; the
church built later on the island was
dedicated to her. The modern translation
of Inchcailloch is the Island of the Old
Woman, but an older meaning of the
Gaelic word *cailloch* is a 'cowled woman',
referring to a nun. From the time of Robert
the Bruce, the island became popular as a
hunting ground for royalty. Inchcailloch
provided the deer with perfect protection
from both wild and human predators.

Today, a regular ferry service runs on
demand all year round from Balmaha
Boatyard, and vessels can be hired if you

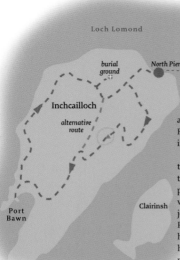

Loch Lomond

Balmaha
visitor
centre
pub
To
Drymen

burial
ground

North Pier

pier

ferry

0   500m

Inchcailloch

alternative
route

Clairinsh

Port
Bawn

are visible along the Highland Boundary Fault, strung out as if hanging from an invisible washing line.

Descend to a junction, turning left along the main path to reach Port Bawn, where there is a pebble and sand beach, and a picnic area. From here, turn right along a walkway, past the toilets and towards the jetty: turn right via the sign for the Low Path before you get to the jetty. The woods here are mainly a mixture of oak, alder and hazel, many of the oaks having been planted to provide bark used to tan leather which was much in demand during the Industrial Revolution. Before this time, much of the island would have been dedicated to growing crops. Today it is a nature reserve and in spring and early summer the ground is a hazy mass of blue from the carpet of bluebells. A ruin on the left is a reminder of the farming that once took place here.

Bear right on a boardwalk and climb to a junction where a short detour straight ahead leads to the churchyard and the site of the church. Although the church fell into disrepair after 1770, local people continued to bring their dead for burial on Inchcailloch until 1947. Back at the junction, turn left to return to the pier and the boat ride back to the mainland.

prefer to make your own way over the water. The charming wooden ferries alight at the north pier, where steps lead up to a path. Bear right into the woods, leaving the shore and reaching an information board and map. Our route turns left onto a rough path to begin the climb to the highest point on the island.

Cross a boardwalk and then follow the path steeply uphill. After a bench, the path goes left to reach a second seat at the summit. This point gives a great view north to the mountains around the head of Loch Lomond. Ben Lomond is the prominent peak to the right. Just a little further along the path, many of the islands

◀ Inchcailloch ferry

Cashel Forest

**Distance 4.5km Time 2 hours
Terrain waymarked woodland paths with
a fair amount of up and down
Map OS Landranger 56 Access no public
transport to start; nearest bus stop is
4km along the road at Balmaha**

**Explore the native woodlands at Cashel
on this straightforward walk with
excellent views over Loch Lomond below
and the chance to visit a reconstructed
shieling – a summer shelter for families
to tend their animals on the hillside.**
    Cashel Estate is owned by the Royal
Scottish Forestry Society, which is
encouraging regeneration of the native

forest in tandem with sustainable working
forestry practices. Because the land rises
steeply from the loch, it contains examples
of most of Scotland's native tree species.
The car park (fee) is signed off the B837,
just north of Balmaha. There is a visitor
centre here which provides more
information about the forest project and
the wildlife and ecology it is helping to
protect. Begin the walk by following the
red waymarkers, turning right after the
visitor centre to pass through a gate and
then aiming for a wooden barn. The route
heads left towards a fence and then a stone
barn where traditional woodworking skills
are demonstrated in the summer.

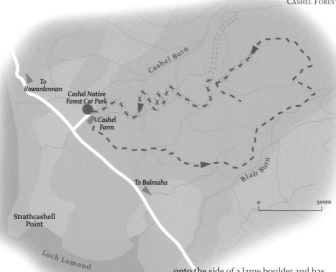

Enter the woods, soon bearing left through young trees. The species here are a mixture of birch, alder, hazel, juniper, oak, Scots pine, yew, aspen and rowan. Keep to the red waymarkers at each junction; the path runs briefly beside a drystone wall before bearing left to cross a burn and then accompany a fence. Go straight ahead at the next junction to shortly reach the reconstructed shieling. These basic structures were used as summer homes for shepherds looking after the flocks out on the hill; sometimes it was the women and children who would spend the summer months on the higher grazing land tending the livestock. This one is built onto the side of a large boulder and has the traditional heather thatch roof.

The route runs across the hillside; at a fork, there is an optional detour to ascend a grassy lump for the best views over Loch Lomond and the numerous islands dotted across the water below. A sculpture, shaped to resemble the early standing stones, is engraved with the words: 'The sun will shine again' – whether this would make you feel better if viewed through thick rain and clag is unclear.

After rejoining the main path, a track is eventually reached. Turn left here to zigzag back down towards Cashel Farm. Just before the car park, you pass an insect 'hotel', designed to provide the perfect habitat for many important species – hopefully not including the midge.

◀ Cashel Farm and Loch Lomond

Ruins of Wester Sallochy

Distance 2.5km Time **1 hour**
Terrain **waymarked forest paths, can
be wet underfoot** Map **OS Landranger 56**
Access **no public transport to start
of walk**

**Sallochy is a stunning spot on the banks
of Loch Lomond. This walk combines two
waymarked trails to climb through the
oakwoods on a visit to the atmospheric
remains of an abandoned settlement and
to look out over the water to the
mountains beyond.**

Sallochy is situated between Balmaha
and Rowardennan on the east side of Loch
Lomond. The car park, with beautiful
places for a picnic, is right on the shore of

the loch. An information board
gives details of the trails: this route
combines the two shorter routes which
are marked in green and blue. Head back
up to the road and cross it, taking the
waymarked path on the far side and
keeping right at the first junction. At the
next junction, again keep right to follow
the green waymarkers.

Soon the abandoned farmsteads of
Wester Sallochy are reached. The roofless
ruins of the stone houses are clearly
visible, though vegetation is slowly
creeping over them. The houses were
abandoned in the 19th century, like so
many places in the Highlands, as landlords
switched their holdings to sheep-farming

◄ The ruins in the forest

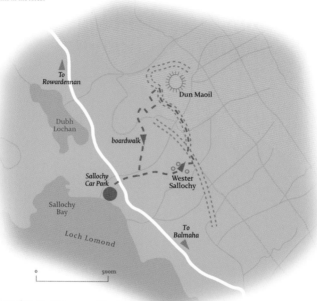

To Rowardennan

Dubh Lochan

boardwalk

Dun Maoil

Sallochy Car Park

Wester Sallochy

Sallochy Bay

Loch Lomond

To Balmaha

0   500m

or, as here, forestry. The encroaching trees make farming life seem like something from a very remote past here.

After an area of fir trees, a track is reached where you turn left. Keep on the main track, bearing right at a junction, and climb towards a crag. Soon a welcome bench provides a fantastic vista over Loch Lomond. Turn left here to follow the blue waymarked route steeply down the bracken-covered hillside.

When the path comes to woodland, turn right onto a grassy track and then bear left to run alongside a fence through lovely oakwoods. A wet section is crossed on a boardwalk before reaching the burn. Turn right to follow it downstream before crossing it on a footbridge. On rejoining the outward route, turn right and head back down to the road and car park.

Sallochy to Rowardennan by the WHW

Distance 4.5km (one-way) Time 1 hour 30 (one-way) Terrain woodland path with some steep sections Map OS Landranger 56 Access no public transport, but in summer a ferry runs to Rowardennan from Inverbeg, where there are regular buses from Glasgow and Balloch

This walk follows a popular and very beautiful section of the West Highland Way along the shores of Loch Lomond. From the far end, you could either have transport arranged or retrace your steps for a new angle on the loch and its varied woodlands. There is a hotel, hostel, car park and toilets at Rowardennan.

Start at the large Forestry Commission car park at Sallochy Bay on the east side of Loch Lomond. From the shore, take the path heading to the right around the lochside, passing through oakwoods and continuing behind a boathouse and jetty.

The £7m building on the right belongs to Glasgow University's Scottish Centre for Ecology and the Natural Environment and is as impressive architecturally as some of the research that students undertake here – ranging from the effects of climate change to the mysteries of the existence of arctic charr in the loch, possibly a survivor from before the ice age. Groups of researchers can, at times, be seen undertaking field work from small boats. Once past the building, keep on the narrow path which climbs to join a track.

Turn left, following the distinctive thistle logo of the West Highland Way. This is one of the most attractive sections of the long-distance route, which extends for 152km (95 miles) from Milngavie, just north of Glasgow, to Fort William. Soon, take a clearly marked path to the right, which rises steadily through the oak trees before reaching an open area with views of Ben Lomond and, further in the distance on the other side of the loch, the peaks

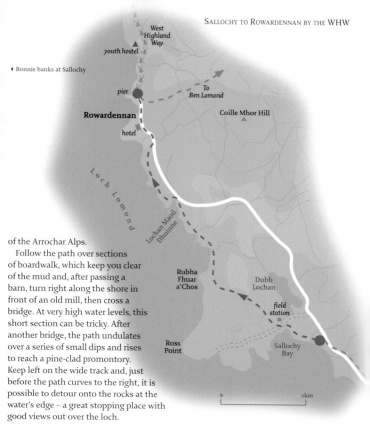

West Highland Way

youth hostel

◄ Bonnie banks at Sallochy

pier

To Ben Lomond

Rowardennan

Coille Mhor Hill

hotel

Loch Lomond

Lochan Maoil Dhuinne

Rubha Fhuar a'Chos

Dubh Lochan

field station

Ross Point

Sallochy Bay

0   1km

of the Arrochar Alps.

Follow the path over sections of boardwalk, which keep you clear of the mud and, after passing a barn, turn right along the shore in front of an old mill, then cross a bridge. At very high water levels, this short section can be tricky. After another bridge, the path undulates over a series of small dips and rises to reach a pine-clad promontory. Keep left on the wide track and, just before the path curves to the right, it is possible to detour onto the rocks at the water's edge – a great stopping place with good views out over the loch.

Keep to the path through the pines until it descends to the road just south of Rowardennan. Turn left to initially follow the pavement alongside the chalet park and then a grassy path to reach the information centre and car park at Rowardennan. This is the end of the public

road on this side of Loch Lomond and is popular with visitors and walkers setting off to bag Ben Lomond, the most southerly of the Munros and the dominant mountain in the area. If a lift has not been arranged, the walk back is well worthwhile for the different views ahead.

63

Ben Lomond from Rowardennan

Distance 12km **Time** 4 hours 30 (round trip) **Terrain** good path, muddy in places, steep climb to summit; the route climbs exposed moorland, so full hillwalking clothes, OS map and navigation skills are essential; alternative descent is boggy and rough; in snow, the ascent is best left to experienced mountaineers
Map OS Explorer 364 **Access** no public transport, but in summer a ferry runs to Rowardennan from Inverbeg, reached by bus from Glasgow and Balloch

Ben Lomond is one of the most popular Munros, rewarding the 30,000 or so people who make it to the top each year with fantastic views of the length of Loch Lomond and its islands, and far into the Highlands to the north and over the Trossachs to the east.

Ben Lomond's status as the most southerly of the Munros (Scottish peaks over 3000 feet) and its accessibility mean that you are unlikely to find solitude here – it is the second most climbed peak in Scotland. Despite this popularity, it is still a tough mountain walk and conditions on the summit are likely to be very different than from the start. Full waterproof kit, good boots, map and compass and the ability to use them are all essential for this walk, and if there is snow on the summits it is best left to the experts.

The climb starts from Rowardennan at the large car park (parking charge) at the end of the public road up the east side of Loch Lomond. There is a small information centre, toilets and, just back down the road, a hotel. A wide, signed path heads uphill immediately behind the information centre. At first, it passes through oakwoods and then a large felled conifer plantation where a project will help encourage the regeneration of native trees. Go straight across a track to continue the climb uphill.

After crossing a small bridge, there are views back over Loch Lomond – these get

better all the time. Pass through a gate onto the open hill, where cattle and sheep graze. Continue the ascent, passing through another gate. This section of path was once a 25m-wide eroded scar, visible for miles, but after extensive repair work undertaken by the National Trust for Scotland, the path is sound and only a couple of metres wide. As the gradient eases, the uppermost slopes come into view with the path visible zigzagging up the right-hand side.

Keep following the broad shoulder of the mountain to reach the steep final ascent to the summit ridge. Here, the route levels off and skirts around the rim of Coire a'Bhathaich, suddenly revealing the unexpectedly craggy and dramatic eastern side of the mountain. From here, the trig point on the summit is just a short walk away and on a clear day the reward is stunning, with views up and down the whole length of Loch Lomond.

The easiest and quickest way back down is to retrace your steps along the path. However, it is also possible to make a circular walk by descending along the Ptarmigan Ridge. This way is much rougher and the path is indistinct and boggy in places. To make this alternative descent, continue past the trig point in a northwesterly direction and climb down a very rocky section of path with care. Once off the steepest ground, the path curves to the left before aiming south along the ridge, eventually dropping alongside a burn to emerge on a track just north of Rowardennan.

◀ Looking towards the islands from the wintry ridge

Ardess Hidden History Trail

Distance 3km **Time** 1 hour
Terrain easy but rough and narrow paths, some uphill, only partial waymarking; a great walk for children, but not suitable for buggies **Map** OS Landranger 56
Access no public transport, but in summer a ferry runs to Rowardennan from Inverbeg, where there are regular buses from Glasgow and Balloch

Head beyond the road end to explore Loch Lomond's wilder side, once the site of an active farming community, and look out for archaeological clues hidden beneath the heather, bracken and oaks.

Follow the road along the east side of Loch Lomond to the large car park at Rowardennan (parking charge) at the end of the public road. From the jetty, the shoreside path travels north. A granite ring sculpture by Doug Cocker frames a lovely view of the north end of the loch. The whole area is a memorial park to Scots who made the ultimate sacrifice during the Second World War. The path soon reaches a track, part of the West Highland Way, where you turn left and then keep right to pass the entrance to the youth hostel. Bear left at the next fork and then turn right up the drive to the Ardess Ranger Centre. Keep to the left of the building where you can pick up a leaflet about the trail. Once behind the building, head uphill to the right, passing the stone-built kennels below – a reminder of the youth hostel's origins as a 19th-century hunting lodge.

As the track climbs, turn right at a corner to go through a gate and join a wooded

◄ Ben Vorlich through the sculpture

path. The oakwoods were planted to satisfy demand for charcoal and for bark used to tan leather. Leather was in short supply at the start of the Industrial Revolution as it was used for the belts that drove machinery in factories springing up all over the country. After a second gate, turn right and go through a third gate. From the track beyond, evidence of ridge and furrow planting can be seen on the far side of the fence.

Soon, you need to bear left uphill, aiming for a lone tree with a seat nearby. An old stone dyke leads you across the open ground, passing the ruins of shielings where people would have lived during the summer months to tend grazing animals. At the far end of the ruins, look for the red markers which direct you downhill towards a gate into the woods. The path wanders through the woodland and then, on open ground once more,

passes the remains of a turf house, and goes through a gate.

After crossing a bridge over the Ardess Burn, turn right to pass the stone ruins of two houses and then climb the bank and through a gate, passing a traditional longhouse, to reach a path which descends from the hillside. Bear left down the path to meet the track, turning left here to return to Rowardennan.

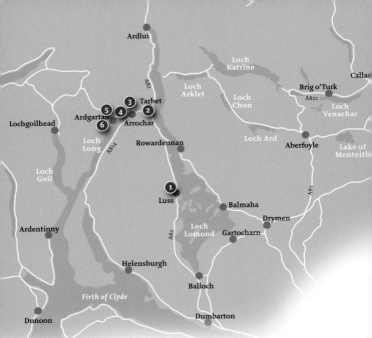

The main road to the Highlands races up the western side of Loch Lomond, but there are plenty of places to stop and admire the fine views across the water and the increasingly steep land rising above. The village of Luss may have been built to house slate-workers, but today its single-storey cottages spilling down to the pier are truly picturesque and it has become a magnet for visitors. Inland is quiet Glen Luss, enclosed by green and shapely hills.

Further north, the loch narrows, its waters hemmed in by true mountains.

Ben Lomond dominates the opposite shore whilst Ben Vorlich towers directly above the road and almost blocks the route onwards. From Tarbet, a narrow isthmus gives an escape route across to Arrochar at the head of Loch Long. Here, the mountains are even rockier and steeper, with so distinctive an appearance that they have become known as the Arrochar Alps. The Cobbler is the best known, though not the highest, its remarkable triumvirate of rocky peaks an icon for travellers and a popular objective for hillwalkers.

From the slopes of Beinn Dubh ▶

West Loch Lomond and Arrochar

Luss and Beinn Dubh

Distance 2.5km (add 6.5km for Beinn Dubh) **Time** 1 hour (add 3 hours for Beinn Dubh) **Terrain** waymarked paths and minor roads around village. The optional ascent of Beinn Dubh crosses steep, open ground: hillwalking clothes, map and navigation skills needed
Map OS Landranger 56 **Access** Luss is well served by buses from Glasgow, Balloch, Crianlarich and Tarbet

This exploration of the historic village of Luss and its environs on the banks of Loch Lomond gives a fascinating insight into how people used to live and work here. Early in the walk, there is the option of climbing to the summit of Beinn Dubh to take in fantastic views of the lochs and mountains for miles around. This detour adds three hours to the route and involves 600m of ascent.

Start from the large car park (summer fee) in the village of Luss and walk along the main road towards the centre. Cross the road, passing the primary school and turning right up a path to cross a footbridge over the busy A82. On the far side, a stile on the right gives access to the Beinn Dubh hill path.

For this strenuous but rewarding detour, climb the grassy path to the gate into the woods. Stay on the main path, keeping left at a fork and following the line of the broad ridge. After shadowing a fence for a while, the path crosses at a stile and eventually reaches a cairn marking the summit, with magnificent views over Loch Lomond's islands and to the Arrochar Alps in the other direction.

To complete the village circuit without the hill detour, ignore the stile to the right and continue ahead until you reach a left turn (SP Quarry Walk). After crossing the road, go through the gate into pretty woodland. Keep on the main path, descending steps to a bridge over the Luss

◀ Beinn Chaorach
from the slopes of
Beinn Dubh

Water. Piles of spoil
from the slate quarry
can be seen on either
side of the river here.
The village of Luss
was built to house
workers for this quarry
and the mills which
can be seen further
down the river on the far
side. The original houses
were low turf-thatched
cottages, often with no
chimneys. The model village seen
today was built around 1850 by the
laird and local clan chief to improve
the conditions of the workers.

Take the path to the left after the
bridge and walk downstream,
passing under the A82 to
accompany the path alongside
livestock fields before reaching the village
road. Cross the road and turn left before
soon descending steps to the right (SP
River Path) and turning right onto the path
below. Follow this alongside the river until
it reaches the first houses of Luss. There is
the option here of detouring to the right
over the footbridge to take a circular loop
of the Glebe, traditionally a piece of land
worked by the villagers to provide funds
for the local church; today, a large celtic
cross stands here.

To continue, keep straight ahead and
pass the church; the current building is
19th century, but some of the gravestones
are thought to be well over a thousand
years old. An 11th-century Viking grave is
a reminder of the Viking raids on Loch
Lomond, when longships were dragged
over the narrow isthmus between Arrochar
and Tarbet. Keep to the left to follow the
banks of the loch towards Luss pier, where
boat trips can be taken in the summer.
Turn left before the pier, then right to head
up the main street and right again at the
top to return to the car park.

71

Tarbet and the Viking raid

Distance 2km **Time** 45 minutes
Terrain undulating woodland path, some
sections of boardwalk and slippery tree
roots **Map** OS Landranger 56
Access no public transport to start of
walk; the nearest buses and trains stop at
Tarbet, but walking along the A82 is
dangerous and not recommended

**A pleasant loop through pine and oak
trees with views over Loch Lomond.
A good short walk for children with the
option of visiting a café halfway round.**

Imagine the creak of straining timbers
and the grunts of exhausted men as two
massive Viking longboats were hauled over
the 2km gap between Arrochar and Tarbet

under cover of darkness. Once the thin
daylight emerged, the fearful rallying cry of
Magnus, son-in-law of King Haakon, was
heard ringing out as a series of surprise
attacks took place on the settlements
dotted along the shores of Loch Lomond.
These boats had been rowed from Norway
to undertake similar raids many times
during the 13th century but, in 1263, this
was the first time Loch Lomond had been
breached and the locals living on the
shores and islands found themselves
undefended. The Vikings made their
escape by following the River Leven to
open water where larger boats were
waiting. However, a storm drove the laden
boats ashore at Largs where the Vikings
were met by an angry Scots army. Today

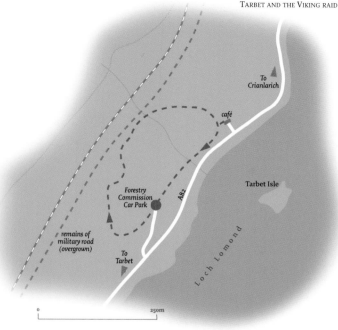

Tarbet and the tiny island named after it are relatively peaceful, the only landing parties being kayakers and fishermen.

Just north of Tarbet, a Forestry Commission-signed track leads up from the A82 to a parking area and the start of the walk. Climb the path towards a stand of Scots pine trees and then curve to the right to head away from the loch. The path meanders through the mixed woodland, following an old stone dyke where the remains of an old military road between Tarbet and Crianlarich can be seen. Once past a gap in the dyke, the route descends towards the café at Blairannaich. Here you can detour over a wooden bridge to refuel at the café or continue on the main path which loops back to the right.

There are glimpses of the water through the oak trees and soon Tarbet Isle comes into view. Only 80m long, the island is privately owned and takes its name from the narrow sliver of land blocking Loch Lomond from Long Long at Arrochar. Soon the path emerges from the trees back at the car park and the start of the walk.

◀ The pine-clad Tarbet Isle

Glen Loin from Arrochar

Distance 17.5km **Time** 4 to 5 hours
Terrain rough forestry tracks and clear
footpaths, steady ascent and descent
Map OS Landranger 56 **Access** regular
buses from Glasgow to Arrochar

**This long exploration of Glen Loin takes
you into the heart of the Arrochar Alps
with a real 'get away from it all' feel.
Despite the length and remoteness, the
going is straightforward.**

Start from the large Loch Long car park in
Arrochar at the head of the loch (fee). Cross
the main road and then take the track that
begins just east of the river, signed for
Forest Walks and Cowal Way. Shortly, at an
information board, branch onto a signed
path to the right, before reaching the
farmhouse. Keep left on joining a bigger
path and continue up the glen. The

mountains of Beinn Narnain and A'Chrois
form an impressive wall to the left.

You may share the path with mountain
bikers, runners and even people out to pan
for gold. Cross the Loin Water on a
footbridge and climb up, shadowed by a line
of pylons. The massif of Ben Vorlich comes
into view ahead as you go through a gate to
reach a high point before descending
towards the trees and then emerging in a
more open area of the next glen.

Follow the main path here, curving to
the right to cross the bridge over the
Inveruglas Water and reach the private road
leading to the Sloy Dam. At this junction,
the route parts company with the Cowal
Way, which turns right to its finish at
Inveruglas. The Cowal Way stretches for
92km from Portavadie, which can be
reached by ferry from Tarbert at the end of
the Kintyre Way. A ferry from Inveruglas
enables the end of the route to link to the

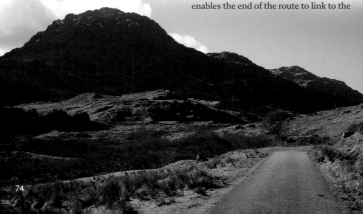

West Highland Way, and with the Great Glen Way beyond that: you can now walk from the Mull of Kintyre to Inverness, all on established long-distance footpaths. Putting such an epic aside for now, turn left and follow the tarmac road. Fork left onto a track at a junction; the road on the right bound for the Sloy Dam is often used to approach Ben Vorlich, so it is common to see tired walkers descending this way. The Sloy Dam holds the dubious honour of the heaviest rainfall recorded in Britain, when 238mm fell in a 24-hour period in January 1974. Today, the rain is put to good use as the dam helps power the nearby hydro-electric powerstation.

Keep to the track as it begins a steady climb up the east side of Coiregrograin. The Munros of Beinn Narnain and Beinn Ime can be seen up the glen, whilst the very steep Ben Vane rises on the right. The track crosses a sluice gate at the highest point in the walk, goes through a gate and makes a gradual descent through forest.

Just before reaching a dam, turn left onto a path to cross a (usually dry) ford and pick up the track again on the other side, now heading left. Soon the track curves right to return down Glen Loin, with Ben Lomond appearing as a sharp peak from this

direction. Pass high above the houses at Succoth before turning sharp left at a junction to double-back down to the bottom of the glen. Head across the flat glen floor on a straight track, keeping with it as it turns right and leads to Succoth. Go left at the T-junction and then take a path to the right just before the telephone box: this leads to a footbridge and then the main A83. Cross the road and follow the path opposite to return to the car park.

◂ Ben Vane from the dam road

Succoth forest loop

**Distance 3.75km Time 1 hour 15
Terrain good tracks and paths, uphill
zigzag section Map OS Landranger 56
Access regular buses from Glasgow
to Arrochar**

**Climb above Loch Long and enjoy superb
views on this straightforward circular
walk at the foot of the Arrochar Alps.
The route finishes with a gentle descent
into peaceful Glen Loin.**

Start from the large car park (fee) just
off the A83 at the western edge of Succoth,
just around the head of Loch Long from
Arrochar. The walk is waymarked in blue
and begins across the road, marked by a
wooden sculpture. This is also the start
for the popular ascent of The Cobbler and
can be busy.

Climb the wooded hillside, which soon
becomes more open, in a series of wide
zigzags. There are good views back over

Loch Long as the ascent continues to a
track beside a bench. The hardest part of
the walk is over, so have a break and enjoy
the view across the loch to the prominent
peaked summit of Ben Lomond which
appears through a gap in the hills.

The length and depth of Loch Long has
led to its use by the Royal Navy for torpedo
testing and submarine operations. The
west shore of the loch just along from
Succoth was used as a base for torpedo
tests between 1912 and 1986. Torpedoes
were fired either from submarines or from
a specially adapted Puffer-type ship. The
range played an important role in
developing these weapons during the
Second World War. In 1944, 12,565
torpedoes were fired down the loch, an
average of 48 runs per day. The lower
reaches of the loch are still the site of
massive naval bases.

Arrochar itself became a popular tourist

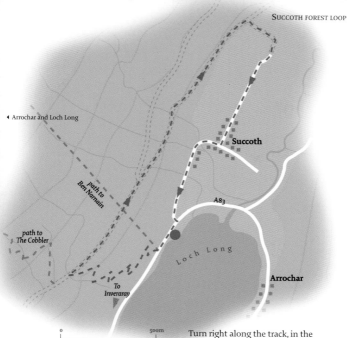

Arrochar and Loch Long ◄

path to Ben Narnain

path to The Cobbler

Succoth

A83

Loch Long

Arrochar

To Inveraray

0   500m

destination when steamers from the Clyde began to run excursions in the 1800s, making accessible places which offered an escape from the cramped urban conditions of Glasgow. In much earlier times, Arrochar was used by the Vikings as a gateway to Loch Lomond. The low valley linking Arrochar with Tarbet, some 2km away on the west side of Loch Lomond, was used in 1263 by Vikings who hauled their longships via the overland route with the intention of raiding the settlements and islands of Loch Lomond.

Turn right along the track, in the direction of Glen Loin. At a fork, take the right branch to begin a gentle descent through the trees. After the barrier, turn right at the bottom of the downhill section to leave the forest. The track now crosses the fields on the floor of Glen Loin. In the middle of the glen, the track bears right and leads to Succoth village, really an extension of nearby Arrochar. Soon the track becomes a road and passes houses on the left. Turn right near the bus stop and then follow the road as it bends left to the A83. Cross the road and go straight ahead to return to the car park at the start.

The Cobbler

Distance 6.75km **Time** 5 hours 30
Terrain steep hill path to summit; the
descent is much rougher with some
rocky sections. Hillwalking gear and
navigation skills needed; as with other
hillwalks, best left to the more
experienced when under snow
Map OS Explorer 364 **Access** regular buses
from Glasgow to Arrochar

The Cobbler, with its bizarre and instantly
recognisable outline, is one of the most
popular hill walks in the area. A great day
out, it ranks amongst the hardest in this
book, but you can shorten the route by
climbing only as far as the Narnain
Boulders. From here, the distinctive rocky
towers can be seen and there are good
views down to Arrochar on
the way back.

The route starts from the
large car park (parking
charge) at Succoth on the
A83 just west of Arrochar.
Cross the A83 and take

the main path, climbing a series of
wide zigzags until you meet a forestry
track. Turn left and then right to reach
the next section of the ascent, with great
views back over the loch to the summit
of Ben Lomond.

The path rises through forestry
plantations before following a burn;
ignore a path off to the right. Soon, the
three rocky summits of The Cobbler come
into view and the path continues its ascent
to reach the massive Narnain Boulders.
The boulders provide rough shelter and
were used as a sleeping and meeting point
for climbers when the Arrochar Alps first
became popular. During the depression
of the 1930s, the area was the haunt of
working-class Glaswegian climbers who
escaped from the shipyards, factories or
dole queues to try out new routes and
push the boundaries of climbing.
Set apart from the traditional
climbers of the professional
establishment, they often based
themselves at the Narnain Boulders

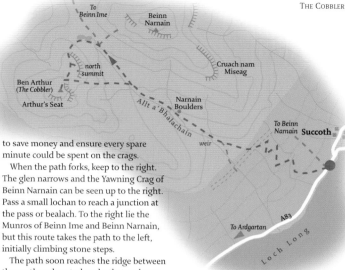

To Beinn Ime

Beinn Narnain

north summit

Ben Arthur (*The Cobbler*)

Arthur's Seat

Cruach nam Miseag

Narnain Boulders

Allt a'Bhalachain

To Beinn Narnain **Succoth**

weir

A83

To Ardgartan

Loch Long

0   1km

to save money and ensure every spare minute could be spent on the crags.

When the path forks, keep to the right. The glen narrows and the Yawning Crag of Beinn Narnain can be seen up to the right. Pass a small lochan to reach a junction at the pass or bealach. To the right lie the Munros of Beinn Ime and Beinn Narnain, but this route takes the path to the left, initially climbing stone steps.

The path soon reaches the ridge between the north and central peaks that make up Ben Arthur, as The Cobbler is also known. Head right to visit the higher, central peak. Here, the true summit is actually a rock pinnacle; experienced scramblers with a good head for heights go through a hole in the pinnacle and then edge around an exposed, slippery ledge before climbing up the far side. Others will have their hearts in their mouths just watching people attempt this, as the wait while they are out of sight is nervewracking.

Retrace your steps to the gap between the central and north peak. From here, you can continue straight ahead and then keep left around the back of the peak to emerge at the lower north summit above a heady overhang. Return to the gap once more, looking out for a cairn of stones marking

the start of the stony descent path. This route is rough and the easier option is to return by the outward path. The advantage of this steeper path heading south from between the north and central peaks is the tremendous view looking up to the mighty cliffs. It is easy to see how these crags fired the imagination of early pioneer climbers who often set off armed only with hob-nailed boots and lengths of washing line.

Keep following the path, which passes through some boggy areas and a couple of rocky sections before improving and crossing the burn to rejoin the main path. Keep right here to retrace your steps to the start.

◀ The Cobbler's summit pinnacle

Ardgartan and the shores of Loch Long

Distance **3.5km** Time **1 hour**
Terrain **minor road, tracks and narrow shore and woodland paths**
Map **OS Landranger 56** Access **regular buses from Arrochar stop opposite the campsite entrance, as do coaches en route to Campbeltown**

This gentle ramble explores both the shores of Loch Long and the wooded banks of the Croe Water at the foot of the Rest and Be Thankful pass.

At Ardgartan, the main A83 road leaves the shores of Loch Long for the steady climb up to the Rest and Be Thankful pass. On the left, soon after leaving the lochside, is the Ardgartan Visitor Centre, run by the Forestry Commission and marked by a large wooden carving of a golden eagle. As well as a car park and waymarked walks, there is a wealth of

local information and a large picnic area. Take the minor road across the bridge, turning left on the far side and following signs for the Coilessan Events Car Park and the campsite: you are walking part of the long-distance Loch Lomond and Cowal Way here. Keep to the blue marker posts as the road gently undulates through attractive mixed woodland. Ignoring a fork off to the left, you will eventually pass the entrance to a campsite. Beyond this, keep an eye out for a path on the left marked with a blue post. This leads downhill to Loch Long, where it then follows the shoreline to the left below the campsite.

After crossing a slipway, the path passes an old boathouse. The views across the loch are idyllic and there is a small beach which makes an ideal spot for a break. The loch contains many wrecks from its time as a torpedo-testing range; these days it is more

◀ Shore of Loch Long

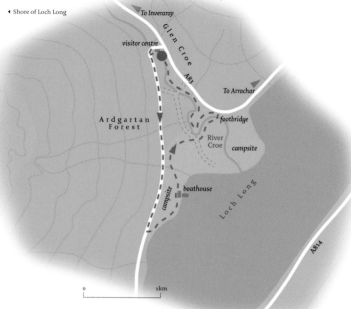

peaceful and the wrecks have become popular with divers. Carry on beside the loch until you meet a clear junction. Turn left here to reach and cross a small bridge; the path then twists and turns through the woodland before reaching a track.

Turn left briefly onto the track, soon veering left onto a narrow footpath beside the river, just before a small group of houses. The riverside path eventually reaches a wooden bridge across the Croe Water. Cross this and climb the bank on the far side, turning immediately left

rather than heading towards the telephone box. This path accompanies the Croe Water upstream, although initially it keeps high above it amongst impressive beech trees. Follow the red and blue marker posts, staying left at a junction to shadow the river closely.

The path eventually merges with a larger one; turn left beyond this and then bear right at the next junction to remain on the same side of the river. Finally, you'll reach the large grassy picnic area of the visitor centre, with the car park just beyond.

Cowal is the forgotten corner of the National Park. Divided from the rest of Argyll by the great sea lochs of Loch Long and Loch Fyne, the approach to this neglected peninsula is over the Rest and Be Thankful pass from Arrochar, or by taking a ferry across the Clyde to the faded resort of Dunoon. Cowal is a rugged place with steep mountains and narrow, densely forested glens, but there are hidden gems here which repay the effort required to seek them out.

The centrepiece of the region is freshwater Loch Eck, with Beinn Mhor rising steeply above and giving its name

to the great botanical gardens at its foot. There are scores of walks in the woods and forests here, with the enchanting Puck's Glen a focal point; in the days of the Clyde steamer, visitors were ferried by horse and cart from Dunoon. Strone Hill rises steeply above the mouth of the Holy Loch, and the coast can be followed round and up the shores of Loch Long to reach pretty Ardentinny. Lochgoilhead, at the tip of a watery finger of Loch Long, was once another port of call for the steamers, but these days is reached only by roads high over the passes.

Holy Loch shores at Kilmun ▶

Cowal

Glen Donich from Lochgoilhead

Distance 4km **Time** 1 hour 30
Terrain good waymarked paths with some
uphill sections **Map** OS Landranger 56
Access direct buses from Dunoon; buses
from Glasgow, Campbeltown and from
Helensburgh stop at the Rest and
Be Thankful

Lochgoilhead enjoys a fine position at the
head of Loch Goil, hemmed in by steep
mountains and accessible only via a high
road over the hills. This waymarked
forestry trail makes an enjoyable circuit of
the lower part of Glen Donich, climbing
above the village to give good views over
the loch and the surrounding mountains.

Start from the centre of the village where
there is a large waterfront car park. From

the late 19th century until the Second
World War, steamboats brought thousands
of holidaymakers from Glasgow and the
Clyde Estuary to Lochgoilhead. Today it
requires a little more effort to reach, but it
remains a popular centre for visitors. Cross
the road and head up the lane signed for
the toilets. After passing these and some
houses, the lane bears left and becomes a
clear path; go through a gate and turn right
up the small track.

Turn left onto a path just before a
wooden bridge, ignoring the sign for the
Duke's Pass, to meet another track slightly
above, with a gate. Go through the gate, but
then continue uphill on the other side of
the fence. From here, the route is marked
by red marker posts. When another track is
reached at a kissing gate, turn left along it.
There are excellent views from here back

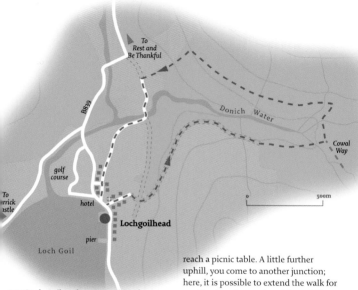

over Loch Goil to the mountains of Beinn Bheula and Beinn Lochain beyond.

Follow the track as it climbs along the edge of the mixed forest. On reaching a gate, cross the stile and carry on into the conifer plantation, now on a clear path. There are occasional glimpses of small waterfalls to the left, and soon the path crosses the Allt Airigh na Creige on a small footbridge. The Loch Lomond and Cowal Way, which has been followed to this point, goes off to the right here, but for this circuit turn left at the junction, as signed for the Forest Walk, and enjoy a beautiful section of path which ascends a flight of steps and crosses the Eas Garbh to

reach a picnic table. A little further uphill, you come to another junction; here, it is possible to extend the walk for another hour by turning right to follow the blue markers which eventually lead to the road along the glen. For the main route, keep left via the red markers as the path starts to head downhill with views across Glen Goil.

Bear right onto a track and carry on down the now open glen. Turn left at the next junction, following the sign for the Glen Donich Circular. Cross the bridge and go straight ahead on the far side. Soon afterwards, turn right to reach the Forestry Commission car park and meet the Lochgoilhead road near the fire station. Turn left here to return along the road to the waterfront car park.

◄ Lochgoilhead

Glenbranter and the Lauder Walk

Distance 4.5km **Time** 2 hours 30
Terrain waymarked paths, some steps and
steep sections **Map** OS Landranger 56
Access no public transport to start –
nearest bus stop for service from Dunoon
is at Strachur, 5km away

**Follow in the footsteps of music hall star
Harry Lauder on this exploration of
Glenbranter Forest. Climb steeply to earn
extensive views of the glen and the head
of Loch Eck before plunging alongside the
Allt Robuic gorge to see its waterfalls and
pools. The walk visits a wildlife hide with
feeders, an excellent spot to watch for red
squirrels and birds.**

Start from the main Forestry
Commission car park in Glenbranter and
not the events car park. The walk initially
follows the green trail and then the yellow:
start by heading back along the track
which led to the car park until you see a
marked path bearing left uphill.

This gives a steady ascent via a series of
zigzags, passing a much needed bench at
the halfway point. Beyond a flight of steps,
the route levels off and contours round to
the left, passing beneath the crags of Creag
Bhaogh. After another bench, the route
climbs again, widens into a track and then
starts to descend. Take a sharp left at a
track junction, continuing downhill and
then veering off to the right on a path
waymarked in yellow. When another
forestry track is reached, turn right again.

During the great depression of the 1930s,
Glenbranter became the site of a notorious
work camp set up by the government to
provide work experience and harden up
unemployed men who some believed had
become soft and unemployable. Although
voluntary, non-attendance for those
selected for the camps meant loss of their
dole money, and many regarded it as
compulsory labour. Although some men
benefited from the three meals a day, they

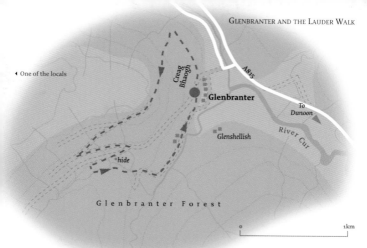

◀ One of the locals

Creag Bhaogh

Glenbranter

A815

To Dunoon

River Cur

Glenshellish

hide

G l e n b r a n t e r   F o r e s t

0   1km

were often made to work 10 to 12 hours daily for 10-week stretches. Many complained that being here made it impossible to hear about any job opportunities back home. Two walkouts were staged in 1935 and 1936, bringing national press attention to the area. During the Second World War, the huts were once again in use, this time to house Italian Prisoners of War.

Soon, a wildlife hide is seen to the left. This is well worth a visit, as feeders attract many red squirrels in addition to numerous woodland birds. Continue to the end of the track, then take the right-hand path which runs along the side of a deep gorge. The trail winds across the steep slope, crossing a number of footbridges and passing a short detour to a viewpoint on the left. This part of the route is named after Harry Lauder, a hugely popular music hall and film star from the

early 20th century, who regularly held massive concerts at his house, Laudervale, and was said at the time to be the highest paid entertainer in the world. His son, who was tragically killed in the First World War, is commemorated by a memorial in the glen where Lauder's wife is buried.

At the head of the gorge, descend steps to reach a waterfall. From here, the route briefly heads downstream and crosses a bridge. Continuing, it eventually comes to a junction of tracks, where you turn left to reach the Ritual Grove car park for disabled visitors and carry on along the main track.

After passing a pair of whitewashed cottages, turn left at the junction (SP Lauder Walks and Wildlife Hide) and then right onto a path at the next corner. Reaching the next junction, turn left over a bridge to pass through woodland above the Forestry Commission buildings and reach the car park at the start.

River Eachaig from Benmore

Distance 7km **Time** 2 hours **Terrain** fairly
level tracks, minor road and rough
woodland paths **Map** OS Landranger 56
Access regular buses from Dunoon –
alight at Benmore Gardens

Explore the plantations and native
woodlands around the Rivers Eachaig and
Massan at the very heart of the Cowal
Peninsula. This walk leaves plenty of time
for a visit to Benmore Botanic Garden.
A couple of bridges ideal for playing
Pooh sticks and a café at the end make it
a good choice for children.

The Botanic Garden at Benmore, 11km
north of Dunoon, is an offshoot of the
Royal Botanic Garden in Edinburgh. In
contrast to the capital's cold climate, the
gulf stream allows more than 300 species
of rhododendron to thrive here, as well as a
magnificent avenue of towering redwoods
and numerous other exotic species
that range over the 140-acre site. The
gardens are Cowal's top visitor attraction;
the café is open to non-garden visitors.
Begin the walk from the Benmore car park,
crossing the main road to bear right along
a track bound for Puck's Glen. After
passing a stone house on the left, turn
right by a decrepit building to follow a
track to the main road. Cross this and
head along the lane opposite to reach
the River Eachaig.

After walking over the bridge, bear
left along the riverside track, keeping on
the main track at a fork and then aiming
right to pass through a gate onto a back
road. Head left, over the River Massan,
and immediately look out for a path
on the right which leads upstream through

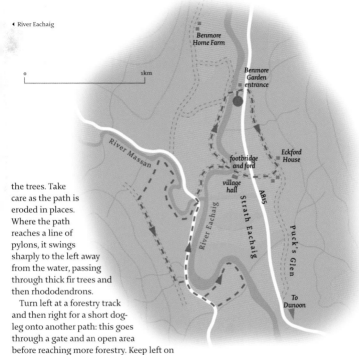

◀ River Eachaig

the trees. Take care as the path is eroded in places. Where the path reaches a line of pylons, it swings sharply to the left away from the water, passing through thick fir trees and then rhododendrons.

Turn left at a forestry track and then right for a short dog-leg onto another path: this goes through a gate and an open area before reaching more forestry. Keep left on the main path, passing through another gate to reach a minor road. Follow the road to the right briefly, shadowing the River Eachaig, whilst looking out for a signed path on the left. This stretch is lovely, skirting the riverbank to reach a small grassy area with a seat. The path continuing ahead is very overgrown, so the best route is to take the path behind the seat and plunge into the dense pines.

Emerge, blinking, back into daylight at the road, turning right to accompany it all the way back to the small bridge over the River Massan crossed earlier. Immediately after the bridge, take the lane on the right to return along the River Eachaig towards Benmore. Instead of crossing the bridge this time, carry on ahead to a roadbridge which leads directly back into the Benmore car park to the right.

Puck's Glen

**Distance 3.5km Time 1 hour 30
Terrain waymarked winding path above
a burn, stone steps which can be slippery
– care needs to be taken with children
Map OS Landranger 56 Access regular
buses from Dunoon to Benmore Botanic
Garden – follow signed footpath to
Puck's Glen**

**Steeped in a magical atmosphere, Puck's
Glen is a short and popular excursion
alongside a tumbling burn. Green moss
hangs heavily from the trees and the
dappled light gives the glen a mystical air.
The walk is made more enchanting by a
series of bridges and stone steps.**

The car park for Puck's Glen is south of
Benmore Botanic Garden, off the A83
heading towards Dunoon. This route
follows the red waymarkers along a section
of the old road at first. After passing the

chalets, turn right up the path signposted
for Puck's Glen.

The path was originally constructed by
the Younger family who owned the
Benmore Estate and are more commonly
associated with their eponymous brewing
company which has been brewing beer in
Scotland in various forms since 1749.
The company merged with McEwans in the
19th century and today is part of the
Scottish and Newcastle giant.

After falling into disrepair, the path was
restored in 1986 and now takes a winding
course up beside the burn, crossing it
many times on wooden footbridges, each
revealing a different view of small
waterfalls and shady pools. The path is
unfenced and there are steep stone steps
in places which can be slippery, so care
needs to be taken and children supervised.

Higher up the glen, the small gorge

◄ The path in the atmospheric glen

deepens and the sides are clothed with dark green ferns and mosses, overshadowed by the dense tree canopy above. After a steep climb, a junction is reached. Here you can turn right to take a shortcut directly back to the car park or continue up the glen. The route descends slightly before heading upstream and crossing yet more bridges. Originally, a decorated hut stood here, typical of the period and the enthusiasm for creating magical atmospheres in places like this. The hut now stands in Benmore Botanic Garden, which is well worth a visit, though a decent amount of time has to be taken to enjoy all Benmore has to offer.

Eventually, the path reaches a forestry track. It is possible to extend the walk by turning left and then choosing any of a number of different paths which all lead back down to the old road. To continue this shorter loop, turn right here and then take the first right onto the return path marked with red waymarkers. If you have the time, you can detour slightly further along the track and turn left to visit a wildlife hide which is well placed overlooking a series of small pools. On the downhill path, a seat is reached, where you turn left to return to the car park.

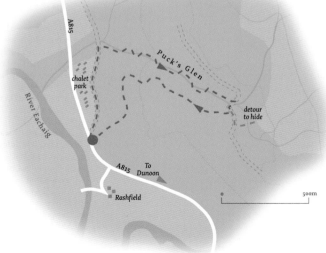

Strone Hill over the Holy Loch

Distance 7.75km Time 3 hours
Terrain steep climb on good paths,
hillwalking gear required
Map OS Landranger 56 Access regular
buses from Dunoon to Kilmun

**Climb steeply above the Holy Loch for
superb views over Loch Long, Dunoon
and the Firth of Clyde, with Arran and the
Cumbraes in the distance.**

There is space to park just east of Kilmun
Pier, opposite the hotel, or alternatively at
the Graham's Point picnic area. Follow the
main road east past Graham's Point,
turning left immediately after Hillside
House into Johnston Avenue. Do not
follow the curve of the road round the
front of the houses, but instead go straight

ahead before turning right to follow a path
which climbs behind them (SP Forest
Walk). At a forestry track, turn left and then
right to gain another gently rising track.
Eventually, this emerges at a clearing above
Strone Point with fantastic views to
Dunoon and down the Clyde as well as to
the Luss hills across Loch Long.

At a fork, leave the track completely and
turn left onto a path which backtracks
uphill, marked by a wooden post. After
shadowing a drystone wall at first uphill,
take the right turn back towards the wall,
then bear left along a narrow and
sometimes muddy path for a steep climb.
Further on, this passes through a gap in
the wall and then continues up the other
side. Cross a small dip and soon the open

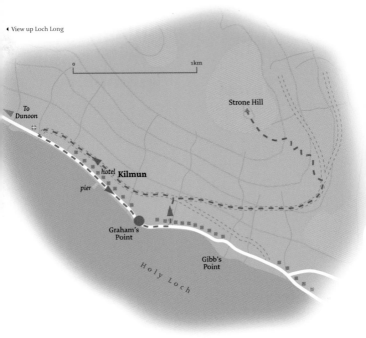

◀ View up Loch Long

summit comes into view. Tramp across the heather to the trig point: the last few metres are pathless and the summit would be hard to find in mist. On a clear day, the islands of Bute, Arran, and Great and Little Cumbrae can all be seen, as well as the mountainous landscapes of the Highlands stretching away to the north.

Return down through the forest, taking care to use the same outward route. Where you meet the forestry track immediately

above Kilmun, keep straight ahead instead of returning down the dog-leg to the left. Soon the track gives lovely views over the Holy Loch, and, further on, joins a concrete drive which leads to the main road. On the right is Kilmun Church with its distinctive dome; the remains of the original church dating from 1422 stand in the grounds whilst inside is a bizarre water-powered organ. To return to the pier, turn left along the pavement.

Ardentinny forest trails

Distance 6km Time 2 hours
Terrain waymarked paths, steep in places,
minor road Map OS Landranger 56
Access regular buses from Dunoon
to Ardentinny

Originally a forestry village, Ardentinny
has a beautiful setting on the shores of
Loch Long. This walk, which is easy to
shorten, links two waymarked trails,
combining great views with the
opportunity to watch for birds and other
wildlife, including red squirrels.

The walk begins at the large Forestry
Commission car park at the north end of
Finart Bay. From the far end, pass the picnic
tables and follow the red waymarkers (SP
Birchwood Walk) to the viewpoint at the
end of the path. Across the otherwise
tranquil waters, the naval base at Coulport
sits in stark contrast. It is a support and
servicing depot for Trident, Britain's
nuclear missile-carrying submarines

which are based at nearby Faslane.

Retrace your steps a short distance and
climb a steep flight of steps to the right
where, instead of crossing the bridge and
carrying on up, you keep to the footpath
ahead, following the red waymarkers.
Another steep ascent is rewarded with
glimpses of the loch between the trees,
before a forestry track is reached. Turn
right here and cross a stone bridge.
When you reach a fork in the track, turn
left to join the blue-marked route
(SP Discovery Trail).

Soon, this comes to a wildlife hide on
the left, positioned in front of stocked
feeders to ensure an almost guaranteed
spectacle of woodland birds or red
squirrels. Although red squirrels are
plentiful in this part of Cowal, nearby Loch
Lomond is the current frontier with the
grey squirrel which is gradually moving
north and driving out the native reds.
The larger greys, which are not native to

hide

path to
Carrick
Castle

To Strachur

Loch Long

Finart Bay

Ardentinny

To Kilmun
& Dunoon

Britain, can live at much higher density than reds, taking up vital habitat and food. However, it is the squirrel pox virus that greys carry that poses the biggest threat to red squirrels, as this virus is always fatal and can wipe out whole colonies, leaving greys to populate the newly cleared area. Various conservation efforts are being made in hotspots such as south Loch Lomond to provide a safe habitat for red squirrels.

After the hide, take the left fork through the woods to a bench where the route loops back to the right and returns to the hide. Continue ahead on the track, going straight on downhill to eventually reach the eagle sculpture at the entrance to the car park. You could end the walk here or continue, following the Laird's Walk which explores Finart Bay and some fine woodland above Ardentinny.

For the Laird's Walk, bear right along the entrance road to the car park. Once over the bridge, take the path which forks left and runs around the back of picturesque Finart Bay. At the end of the bay, the track leads you to a road which you cross to enter a car park in the village itself. Like many place names derived from Gaelic, there is some debate as to the original name and meaning of Ardentinny: it is most likely to come from the Gaelic, Àird an t-Sionnaich, which means the 'Headland of

the Fox', although others maintain it derives from Ard An-Teine, meaning 'Headland of Fire' and refers to the practice of lighting beacon fires as a warning to ships heading up and down the loch.

Take the path from the back of the car park running alongside a burn before diving into the trees. When you reach a forest track, turn right, passing a memorial stone with a bench on the far side and a fantastic view over the bay. The track now drops downhill to join the road; follow this briefly before turning right onto a track with yellow markers. This leads back to the bridge near the entrance to the car park.

◂ Finart Bay

Index